*The first Prioress of Sneaton Castle
Mother Margaret OHP*

Photograph taken by Frank Sutcliffe, 1919

The WHITBY SISTERS

A Chronicle of the Order of the Holy Paraclete, 1915 – 2000

Rosalin Barker

Edited and arranged by Sisters of the Order of the Holy Paraclete

Published by the Order of the Holy Paraclete, Whitby

First published in 2001
by the Order of the Holy Paraclete
Sneaton Castle
Whitby YO21 3QN

All rights reserved

© Order of the Holy Paraclete 2001

ISBN 0-9540617-0-5

A CIP record of this book is available from the British Library

Layout and design by the Order of the Holy Paraclete Publications Group
assisted by Graphic Example, Norton, Stockton-on-Tees

Printed by Billingham Press Limited, Billingham, Stockton-on-Tees

CONTENTS

Foreword		vii
Acknowledgements		viii
Preface		x
Chapter 1	Beginnings	1
Chapter 2	Between the Wars	9
	A Brief History of Sneaton Castle	*17.*
Chapter 3	1940 – 1960	25
Chapter 4	The Sixties and Seventies	41
	The Office of Prioress	*44*
Chapter 5	The End of the Millennium	51
Bibliography		60
Appendix I		61
Appendix II		62

FOREWORD
from the Bishop of Whitby

I first began to know Sisters of the Order of the Holy Paraclete while in the Diocese of Blackburn and some of them were working in the City of Lancaster; I subsequently became Archdeacon of Lancaster. A most helpful early contact was in connection with my work as Chaplain in Bishop Rawstorne School. It is a relationship that has deepened with time and I chose to spend my pre-Consecration Retreat at Sneaton Castle.

As Bishop of Whitby it has been my privilege to share in a number of Community occasions. As I have learned more of the Order I have become increasingly aware of what they have to offer to the Church and the wider community.

This Chronicle of their history adds a fresh perspective on their life and work and their contribution to the Church, not only in the Diocese of York but far beyond it. The story of the pioneering days in Africa reads like an adventure tale and such indeed it was!

This spirit of adventure still characterises the Order and it is my hope that this book will help to make the Sisters more widely known and appreciated.

The Rt Revd Robert Ladds
Bishop of Whitby

Acknowledgements

I am grateful to the Prioress and Chapter of the Order of the Holy Paraclete for enabling me to undertake this short chronicle. It has been an exciting task, giving me considerable insight into their remarkable history and into the ~~world of the religious~~ community in general.

My main source has been the archive of the Order which has been made available to me. Here I must particularly thank Sr Hilary who has guided me through the archive, and Sr Anita, the Chapter Clerk, who has searched the otherwise-closed Chapter minutes for information which I have needed. Sr Catherine has helped me enormously as part of the publications committee, and with her carefully compiled notes of past events.

The sisters came together in August 2000, from all the OHP houses for the millennium Greater Chapter. It was the first time since 1926 that the entire community had been together in the Mother House. They read the drafts, and helped me to put right my errors of fact and ommission, and gave me a much wider insight into the workings of the community.

E-mail has made communications overseas much easier and I have been grateful to Sisters Maureen, Jocelyn and Rosa for their efforts in this field. Many sisters have been accumulating little memoirs of their lives, and adventures, in the Order, and I have thoroughly enjoyed these. Others have endured my long lists of questions with charm and equanimity.

Outside the Order my thanks are due to Aidan Healey, nephew of the Foundress, who was most kind and helpful with information about his parents and aunts; to the Brynmor-Jones Library of the University of Hull, with its collection of obscurer books on the history of education in Africa; to Simon Bailey, Oxford University Archivist, for his patience and help in teasing out the details of Mother Margaret's university education; to York Minster Library for its weighty volumes of early *Crockfords*; to the Archivists at the University of Cambridge, St Anne's, Oxford and the King Edward Foundation, and to the local authority Archivists at Dudley, Wolverhampton and Birmingham. My brother, Malcolm Dunkeld, for many years a senior journalist on the Johannesburg *Post*, has helped with the background on South Africa and with reminders of the dark days of apartheid.

Above all, my family has kept the domestic show on the road, while I worked at my desk or in the south tower at the Castle, and two successive dogs have helped me clear my head with walks.

It has been a humbling experience to observe the courage with which the sisters have set out on their journeys, have adapted and adjusted to civil unrest, political brutality, hunger, war, climate and disease, yet have remained their cheerful, smiling selves when they come back home to St Hilda's Priory at Whitby. My earliest memory of the sisters goes back to a university vacation in the 1950s, and seeing some of them unselfconsciously paddling on the beach at Whitby. There was about them dignity but not a scrap of pomposity.

I have admired them ever since.

Rosalin Barker

Our thanks are due for permission to use copyright material: Colin Waters for the map on page 5, the Church Commissioners for the photograph of Archbishop Lang, the Community of the Resurrection for the photograph of Fr Frere. Assistance has also been received from the Whitby Literary & Philosophical Society Library and the North Yorkshire Archives Department at Northallerton.

Publications Group

Preface

When I was asked whether I would be prepared to write a brief chronicle of the Order of the Holy Paraclete from its foundation in 1915 to the present day, I had been compiling a distance learning anthology for adult students, looking at the social and environmental history of Whitby. This had entailed a considerable search through the evidence on the life of St Hilda, the seventh century Abbess of Whitby. I was at the same time involved with a project to translate the *Cartulary* of the mediaeval Abbey, dedicated to St Peter and St Hilda, whose ruins now stand on the east cliff at Whitby. The Mother House of the Order of the Holy Parclete is also in Whitby, and although the Order is dedicated to the Holy Spirit, the Priory building is dedicated to St Hilda, founded 1258 years after the first Abbey, and 837 years after the second. It has been impossible not to see great similarities between the three houses, and, at the same time, to see differences, some of which are theological, and some simply due to the passage of time.

All three had determined and able founders; Hilda, Reinfrid and Margaret Cope, remembered long after their deaths for their abilities and for the qualities of their characters. All three Houses were founded during or as a result of, conflict. Hilda's Anglo-Saxon name Hild meant 'struggle', and the Abbey which she governed was founded by King Oswy as a thank-offering to God for the defeat of the last pagan king of Mercia. The Benedictine abbey of 1078 was founded as a result of the harrying of the north by King William the Conqueror, which brought Reinfrid into contact with the evidence of the destruction left by the Danes, drew him to monastic life and led him to re-found St Hilda's Abbey. Margaret Cope and her companions came to Sneaton Castle on 5th November, in the first year of the Great War.

This is their story.

Chapter 1 Beginnings

In the history of religious orders it is often the case that the story of a new foundation cannot be separated from the personal story of its founder. This is certainly true of the Order of the Holy Paraclete which began in 1915 under the leadership of Margaret Cope who was Prioress until her death in February 1961.

Margaret Cope: early years

Margaret Cope was born in Oswestry on 2nd October 1886, to Wynn and Margaret Cope. Wynn Cope was then a clerk with the Great Western Railway, and his wife was the daughter of a Shropshire farmer and miller, William Francis. Hence the new baby, the eldest of three, was given the Christian names Margaret Sylvia Francis. As a railway family, the Copes moved around the region served by Great Western, and Wynn Cope finally retired as Station Master at Wolverhampton Low Level Station. In retirement he and his wife returned to Oswestry till his death in 1928, when his widow moved to Whitby. All three children were active, clever, aware, and, as the writer of *Fulfilled in Joy*, Sr Ethel Mary, says, 'characteristically dynamic'.

Education for girls, to any kind of advanced level, was very hit or miss at the turn of the nineteenth and twentieth centuries, but Margaret was fortunate in attending Dudley High School. Sadly, the school records are extant only from 1908. Sr Ethel Mary describes her move to King Edward VI School at Birmingham. Since there is no record of her attendance there as a pupil, it is likely that she went as a pupil-teacher, doing her practical work in the slum schools of Birmingham, sharpening her compassion for the socially disadvantaged.

At some point, presumably when her 'apprenticeship' had been completed, she went to Oxford to acquire some academic qualifications for teaching. She could not, of course, take a degree there as women were barred from Oxford degrees till 1920, but as a 'home student' she was able to study both Education and Geography. The Oxford University Archives contain a letter dated 27th April 1908, from Cherwell Hall, explaining that Margaret Cope and others would attend the lectures of the Reader at the Oxford Secondary Teaching Delegacy. She passed the practical examination for the Cambridge University Secondary Teachers' Diploma in June, 1908. Her examiner's report in the practice of teaching gave her a distinction. As an affiliate at Cherwell Hall, Margaret was awarded the Certificate in Regional and Physical Geography

Margaret Cope, c. 1904

in Trinity Term, 1909. Thus, with her practical experience from her pupil-teacher years and her two qualifications from Oxford and Cambridge she was, although not a graduate, well equipped to enter the expanding world of girls' education.

In her manuscript chronicle of the early years of the Order of the Holy Paraclete, Sr Ethel Mary records that Margaret was offered a post at Oxford as a demonstrator in geography, but declined. Certainly such a post was filled around this time, but there is no direct archival evidence of the offer to Margaret Cope.

> *Miss Margaret S.F. Cope gave a lesson on Norway and Sweden – her manner was light and pleasant. She had copious information and her drawings and blackboard work were good. She kept good discipline and the class was interested. I should award her distinction.*
>
> Transcript of Margaret Cope's practical examiner's report for the Cambridge Secondary Teachers' Diploma, 28th June 1908.

According to a letter from an older fellow student Margaret had now become deeply religious. She had begun to think seriously of overseas mission teaching, and had discussed the idea with Fr Lucius Carey of the Oxford-based Society of St John the Evangelist, the 'Cowley Fathers', who had suggested that she set her sights on the Society's work in India. However, at only 22, Margaret was, in 1909, still too young for the mission field, and in the end a different 'call' came.

Society of St Peter, Horbury

Horbury was then a small community lying south-west of Wakefield, on the road to Huddersfield. There, in 1858, the Society of St Peter had been founded, dedicated to the reform of those women who had succumbed to the appalling poverty and crime of the congested mill town slums. Its work among the abused and dispossessed had been greatly respected over many years. It was not a teaching Society, but had opened St Hilda's School for girls, a day-school which became a small high school, in 1875 in Horbury. In 1905 the community opened another school in Nassau, in the Bahamas, and in 1912, St Margaret's School, at Tonge Moor in Lancashire.

In September, 1908, a fellow-student from Cherwell Hall, Katherina Rein, daughter of a professor at the University of

Jena, left for Horbury, to take over St Hilda's School, and to build it up to cope with increasing numbers. In 1909 she invited Margaret Cope to join her as second mistress until she was old enough to serve in missionary work.

Already at Horbury was Edith Mary Healey, born in 1880, who had taught, unqualified, in the school for three and a half years, before becoming a postulant in January 1908, and being clothed as a novice four months later, taking the name Mary Edith. She was professed as a sister in November 1910. Because of Mary Edith's skills as a teacher, Katherina Rein, using her father's contacts, arranged with the University of Leeds for an inspection which led to the school's being approved for the training of pupil-teachers, and presumably thus enabled Mary Edith to achieve qualified status.

Margaret Cope succeeded Katherina Rein as head of the school in 1910, when her colleague was accepted by the Society as a postulant and was withdrawn from the school, which continued to flourish under Margaret Cope. The following year, the annual report of the Superior records the opening of a second girls' school, St Margaret's, at Tonge Moor in Lancashire, where the Sisters were already involved in parish work. There was no annual report in 1912 owing to the Superior's serious illness; by 1913 St Margaret's School had disappeared from the annual report.

In 1912, Margaret Cope herself became a postulant, at the age of 25, and then a novice, under her middle name of Sylvia. She continued to run the school, but there were already rumblings within the Society as to whether its true function was teaching or penitent work, especially, one suspects, during the serious illness of the Superior, Mother Margaret SSP. In fact, at this precise time, Novice Katherina Rein left the Society of St Peter and joined a teaching order, the Community of the Holy Family, in London. It is also possible that these concerns about the work of the Society contained a growing, and perhaps uncomfortable, awareness of the strong personality of Sr Sylvia. The revered and much-loved Mother Margaret SSP, died in 1914, and was succeeded by Mother Anna SSP, and the concerns began to come to a head.

It is possible to trace most of the story from a variety of sources. There is the hand-written chronicle of the early years, which is not contemporary with the events, and contains considerable 'hindsight', but the writers had lived through the events and had access to diaries for some of the years. In addition the Order's archives contain draft letters and actual replies, from a correspondence between Sr Mary Edith at Horbury and the Visitor to the SSP, the Bishop of Wakefield.

Sr Sylvia, c. 1912

Mary Wilkinson, daughter of a mission priest returned from Nassau, and a pupil at both Horbury and Whitby, has also written a short memoir of the early days, and of the dramatic events leading up to the founding of the Order. There is a brief note on the page devoted to Sr Mary Edith in the SSP professions register. Lastly, there is Sr Ethel Mary's account, published in 1964, *Fulfilled in Joy*. When the move from Horbury to Whitby took place, Ethel Mary Greenshaw, later Sr Ethel Mary, was a secular teacher in the school.

Sr Sylvia returned to the school in time for Speech Day at the end of term, as promised, after a period of work with the penitents and at Wakefield prison. Since she had not proceeded to profession soon after her due date, there may have been some hesitation, either on the part of Sylvia herself, or on the part of the Society.

School broke up and, on 4th August 1914, war was declared against Germany. Ethel Greenshaw and another teacher were on holiday in Goathland when a letter arrived from Horbury announcing the closure of the school in December. Yet Mary Wilkinson remembered parents discussing this at the last Speech Day in July, and Sr Mary Edith's letters to the Bishop state that the decision had been finalised at Chapter on September 14th. However, *Fulfilled in Joy* tells of a visit during the school holidays to Rievaulx Abbey, where Sr Sylvia clearly saw her path forward. Thus when Ethel Greenshaw was asked to return to school a few days before term began, she was presented with the idea that there would be a new Order and that the school would move with it.

Horbury staff, 1913

Ethel arranged for a friend who lived in Whitby to send details of premises suitable for a school. The school at Horbury was St Hilda's School, and Whitby was St Hilda's town and known to all the protagonists. It was, as a coastal area, a risky place in wartime, but nevertheless plans moved forward. As far as SSP was concerned, poor Sr Mary Edith bore the worst of the odium associated with the disruption. She had argued in Chapter against closure but had failed to convince the meeting and was thus isolated from her community, the only professed sister living at the school. On the other hand, Sr Sylvia, as a Novice, required no dispensation to leave the Society.

Sr Sylvia, now aged twenty-eight, had confided in her mother, and they, with Ethel Greenshaw, went for the day to Whitby and inspected Sneaton Castle for the first time on a wet 5th November. It had been leased by a Captain Edwards to become a boys' school, but Captain Edwards had re-enlisted, and the Castle was available immediately. *(See pages 17 to 24 for more about the Castle.)*

In great trepidation the group opened negotiations with Colonel Richardson, the owner, for taking over the lease, and faced the problems of raising the necessary money. The response from parents was encouraging, in terms of donations, loans and offers of the goods necessary for opening a school. On 18th November, one month before the school at Horbury was due to close for the last time, Sr Mary Edith first wrote to the Bishop of Wakefield to try to obtain her release from her vows to SSP. The Bishop dealt carefully with this serious dilemma; he offered advice; he took evidence; agreed that there was wrong on the side of the Society, but said that in breaching Chapter confidentiality, Mary Edith had transgressed against the Rule. After a month of meetings, carefully-written letters and a great deal of consultation, Mary Edith was released from her vows as the School finally closed.

It says much for the Bishop's skill that Sr Mary Edith was able to say that the atmosphere in her last days at Horbury was much happier. She had no wish to damage the Society of which she had been a member for six years, four of them in profession. During this period much had been done towards the moving of the school, and the preparation for the new Order, including preparing habits for Sr Sylvia (who now reverted to her first name of Margaret) and Sr Mary Edith.

The day they left Horbury, the two sisters made their intention to God at St Mark's, Leeds, where Fr Wilkinson acted as curate. Present at the service was a small group of friends, including the three secular teachers who had left Horbury with them, Ethel Greenshaw, Alice Bates and Enid Dawson. It had been decided that the new Order should be dedicated to the Holy Spirit. It was a momentous day, not only for the small party, but also for their destination, for it was on that day that six German warships bombarded the north-east coast, causing damage and loss of life at Scarborough, Whitby and Hartlepool.

The three secular staff also intended to test their vocations in the new Order, though one subsequently remained a secular teacher, and four other secular staff from Horbury had offered to move with the school.

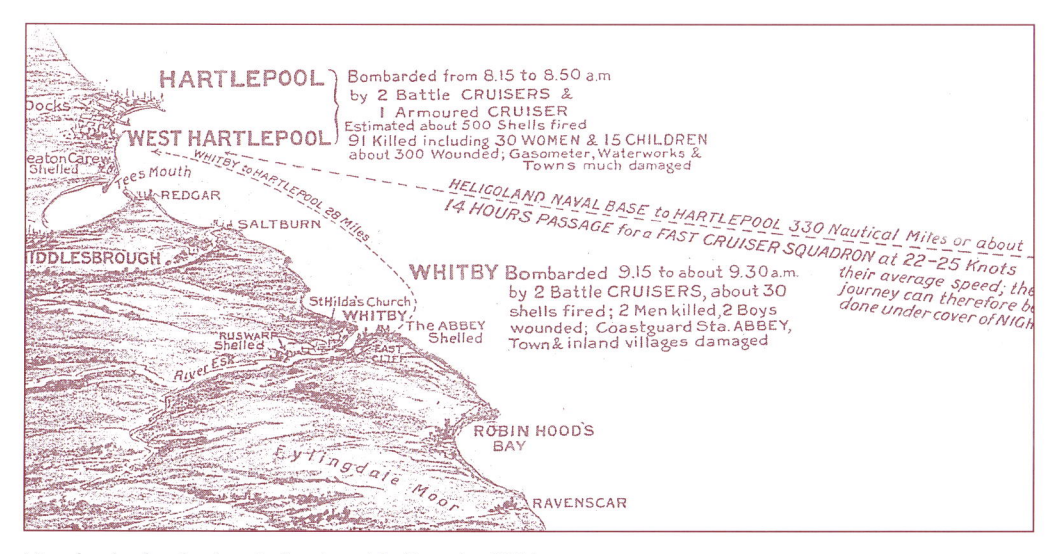

Map showing bombardment of east coast in December 1914

The Whitby Sisters   **Beginnings**

A new life in Whitby

Next day, 17th December, the party split up, Sr Margaret and Ethel Greenshaw to go to Whitby to make the final decisions and arrangements. Then Ethel went home to Hull and Sr Margaret rejoined Sr Mary Edith, to spend Christmas with Sr Margaret's parents at Wolverhampton, working hard on preparations for the school.

On 1st January 1915, Sr Mary Edith went to Whitby to be joined next day by Sr Margaret. The Castle was cold and sparsely furnished: wartime made all supplies short and domestic staff were difficult to find, for there was little money to pay them. Yet there was a tremendous sense of purpose; furniture was given and a chapel – essential for the new Order – was created in the south tower. They went to daily Mass at St Ninian's Church in Whitby, and the Sarum Breviary was used for the daily offices of the Order. One of the secular staff arrived and was admitted as a postulant, called Sr Alice.

Work began on a Constitution for the Order; classrooms and dormitories were prepared, and, on January 29th, 32 pupils who had been at Horbury arrived at the new school. There is in the Order's archives a series of Annual Reports for St Hilda's School, and these progress seamlessly from the school at Horbury to the school at Whitby. That of 1914 made no mention of the closure of the school at Horbury. That for 1915 simply carries on with the new status quo. This was not a **new** school, simply a new **location**, and a new teaching Order administering it. Most of the pupils were the same, as were most of the staff.

Three days after the school opened, Sr Margaret travelled to York to meet Archbishop Cosmo Gordon Lang for the first time. Sr Ethel Mary reports that during their discussions the Archbishop suggested that perhaps at twenty-eight she was rather young to be founding a new Order! Sr Margaret responded by pointing out that it was said that he was rather young to be an Archbishop! He was then, several years into his primacy, only fifty. In the end Archbishop Lang proved sympathetic. He had done his research, and he placed the embryonic Order under Canon George Austen, Rector of Whitby and Chancellor of York. As Sr Ethel Mary writes: "He allowed the co-option of new members, licensed the Chapel and finally bestowed his episcopal blessing on Sister Margaret and her enterprise."

Archbishop Lang's portrait by William Orpen

Garden Fete Committee, 1923. The Order had begun to host such events during the 1914-18 War

Whitby was less sure; traumatised by the bombardment which had been thought to herald an invasion, the inhabitants feared the nuns were German spies, and that the packing cases of children's belongings and school equipment contained armaments. It was some time before the town was convinced by the everyday presence of the children.

The next few months were trying: wartime shortages, impatience with delay in recognition of the Order, which would allow the taking of profession vows (Sr Margaret was still only a Novice), plans for building and adaptation to accommodate the school, drafting a Rule and Constitution for the proposed Order and staffing problems. At the same time work in the town, the start of the annual fetes for local needs and fire-watching against zeppelin raids all made life hard.

Sr Margaret's tendency to asceticism made the first Lent a trial to the postulants, especially when added to wartime shortages. At first most of the Castle lighting was by carbide gas, although by 1918 electricity was installed. There was some central heating, but the gardener-handyman who cared for the boiler refused to work on Sundays!

Eventually Canon Austen permitted Sr Margaret to approach the Archbishop again in July and he replied, appointing Dr Walter Frere, Superior of the Community of the Resurrection at Mirfield, to be the new Order's spiritual adviser. It was an inspired choice. The complexities of Fr Frere's task are explained in *Fulfilled in Joy*, and the work of CR itself is ably described in Anson's *The Call of the Cloister*. The Rule and Constitution passed to and fro, as did anxieties about the Order's name, the lectionaries and the horarium, until by August 1917 the Archbishop finally accepted the new Order of the Holy Paraclete, and became its first Visitor.

Walter Howard Frere CR

The Foundation of the Order

On 16th October 1917, now regarded as Foundation Day, the first professions took place, two weeks after Margaret Cope's 31st birthday and twenty months after the departure from Horbury. Novice Margaret made her first profession together with Novices Ethel Mary and Alice; Sr Mary Edith registered her vow of obedience to the new Order, and the newly professed Sr Margaret was installed as first Prioress, Mother Margaret. The service was conducted by the Archbishop, and the same day Fr Frere retired as Spiritual Adviser, handing over to the Revd Frederick Drake, Rector of Kirby Misperton. A strong link with the Community of the Resurrection at Mirfield has continued since.

Changes and developments

During the Great War the school was slowly developing; public exams were taken by the older pupils, who took part in much of the religious life of the community – that was, after all, part of the ethos of the school; new staff came and went, and as broad a curriculum as was possible was introduced. There was strong emphasis on Games and Drill. Sr Ethel Mary's chronicle and surviving diaries detail events. A tradition of hospitality grew and many came to stay, some to test a vocation, not always successfully, some to participate in community retreats. Gifts of vestments and other items were made to enhance the worship in the chapel, plans were laid for additional buildings in the disused stables, and a fund was started for a proper chapel. The links with St Ninian's were strong and Fr Hart, the priest-in-charge, began to come to the community to celebrate Mass at least once a week.

By 1918, there had been many developments. Two other Sisters had been professed; Revd Gerald Healey, Sr Mary Edith's brother, became the Order's first Chaplain, and in 1919 married Mother Margaret's younger sister Gwen.

In 1918, Rupert Deakin, MA, sent a report to the Local Examinations and Lectures Syndicate of the University of Cambridge, detailing his inspection of the school, in very humane terms. He described classes, the excellent self-discipline of the pupils and the high qualifications of the staff. He also listed the accommodation, though there is a footnote that there was no laboratory or art room. At the head of his list of further details are the words, 'St Hilda's School has been recognised by the Cambridge University Syndicate as a Training Department for secondary teachers.' This was because of its continuity from Horbury. In fact, as early as 1916 the first of a series of pupils left the school at Whitby to return as a student.

The report also records the fees, and the new buildings under construction, and the fact that Stakesby Manor had been rented for staff and senior pupils. *(See Appendix I for full report.)* The school had weathered the usual childhood epidemics, and several cold winters, and had begun the tradition of producing plays and concerts to which the local population was invited. These raised funds for good causes, despite the pressing needs of the Order's overdrafts. The parliamentary election held immediately after the ending of the war showed the strong influence of the Christian Socialist tradition; Sr Ethel Mary reported that most of the sisters voted for the Labour candidate, Mr Rowntree.

In 1919 permission was obtained from Colonel Richardson, the landlord, to build a Chapel (which is now Sneaton Castle Centre's refectory) and also the necessary laboratory. Stakesby Manor was abruptly abandoned; the landlord removed the roof! New arrangements were hastily made for the senior girls. More sisters were professed, and others who had tested their vocations left. A decision was taken at Chapter in 1919 to accept any work which was offered overseas. The Order was ready to face the wider world. Their good friend Canon Austen retired to York; Mother Margaret's first term as Prioress expired and she was re-elected; the first pupils departed to University, to King's College, London. Pupils took part in the Eskdale Tournament, a Whitby music festival which attracted entrants from a wide area, and which still occurs annually. A new charitable venture was begun: the purchase and support of 'Hilda', a cow. Hilda's function was to provide milk for German babies in a distressed area and each form in the school put on a performance to raise the money for this project.

This was no inward-looking community.

Chapter 2   Between the Wars

The Order in Whitby

That so much had been achieved by the Order, and that they had been accepted by the Archbishop, says much about the way attitudes within the Anglican Church had changed since the first community of sisters, the Sisterhood of the Holy Cross, had been founded in 1845. In fact it was not until 1908 that the episcopal hierarchy of the Church of England finally bestowed some kind of official sanction on the Anglican women's communities. 'Regular' life for women had been largely accepted; the Communities followed Anglican doctrine and practice, but, despite the presence of male

> ### State of the Order in 1920
>
> *At the end of 1920, there were in the Order, the Prioress, Mother Margaret, Sr Mary Edith, who had made her life vows years before in Horbury, and five others – Sisters Ethel Mary, Alice, Mabel, Dorothy and Faith who had made a first profession; there were also six novices. The Order had acquired a Chaplain, as well as its Spiritual Adviser, but the Chapter, of professed sisters, managed itself, without the usual appointment of a male Warden. It had His Grace as Visitor, but the Chapter ran itself. The school, too, was self-running. The girls elected their own prefects, and arranged their own discipline. They were, after all, set an excellent example of what clever and right-thinking women could do for themselves and for the religious life to which they were dedicated.*

Chaplains, Wardens, Spiritual Advisers and Visitors, they were self-governing, and independent within the Anglican communion. Susan Mumm's book, *Stolen Daughters, Virgin Mothers* gives an excellent account of the development of the early orders, and their struggles out of the rigidity of Victorian society.

At last, in 1921 came the day, on July 2nd, when the founding sisters were able to make their Life Professions in the Order, in their new Chapel of the Holy Paraclete. From then, until 1965, that became the norm for the Order; the Novitiate of between two and three years was followed by Life Profession. In the turbulent times of the mid-sixties the Constitution was changed so that, from 1966 to 1972, a First Profession of five years was instituted, altered in 1972 to three years with a possibility of renewal for one, two or three years, followed by Life Profession. This practice has continued to the present day. Meanwhile, Archbishop Lang was concerned about security of tenure in the still-rented Castle, and it was also a concern to the sisters, who were putting their own money into improvements, as well as paying rent. This was no richly endowed Victorian Order of gentlewomen who could bring either capital or income, or even family jewels, when they joined. The founders were school teachers, who had come with tiny funds, loans and donations in kind to supplement the school fees, for their support.

In 1923 the bachelor Colonel Richardson died, having disentailed the property, and the sisters were able to buy the Castle from his heir, on a mortgage. Despite the anxiety of repayments, at last the Order owned its home, and any improvements the sisters made were for themselves. In 1923 Mother Margaret was re-elected as Prioress, in time for the handing over of the Castle.

The Church's Task-force

The next year, 1924, they received an invitation from the incumbent at Tonge Moor in Lancashire to assist him in the parish and in a school. It was perhaps his earlier encounter with Horbury which had encouraged him to ask. Thus the first branch house of the Order outside Whitby was opened, and the sisters remained there until 1928, doing work for which the Order was little remunerated and which caused anxious drains upon expenditure. The name of the school is not recorded, but as the problems over finance seem, according to Chapter minutes, to have been caused by lack of fees, and a need for more pupils, it is possible that this was the St Margaret's School, established in Tonge Moor in 1911 by SSP from Horbury, and become by 1926 a problem for the parish. In 1928 the Sisters of the Holy Rood at Middlesbrough agreed to take over the work in Tonge Moor. Holy Rood was a much older, and probably better-funded order.

Nonetheless, the precedent for branch houses in England, and for teaching in other schools, had been established. By the end of the decade there had been half a year spent in a church primary school in Ashington, in Northumberland, and the opening of a house in Newcastle-upon-Tyne, in St Anthony's parish, where the 'house' was in rooms over a butcher's shop. It is worth remembering that at this stage the only other Anglican sisterhoods in the north of England were Holy Rood, a nursing order at Middlesbrough, and Horbury, which had re-opened a girls' day-school but was about to undergo, in 1932, a major split, with most of the Society moving south to Laleham Abbey. The Order of the Holy Paraclete was thus the only teaching order in the north.

In Whitby itself, the Order continued its involvement with the parish, a parish which had sadly been allowed to become fragmented among several chapels of ease. Dinners were given for the unemployed, funds were raised for local welfare, plays and oratorios were performed for the town. Money was also raised for the starving in Russia after the revolution, and for other charities. The Order became involved in missions and missionary events held in the town.

Priory and School

Throughout this decade there were many developments and changes. A cloister was added to the new chapel; a sanatorium was built for pupils. School confirmations were held, and numbers of pupils grew. It is easy in these present egalitarian days, with universally available secondary and higher education for girls, to question whether an Anglican teaching order ought to have been running a private girls' boarding school, and indeed there is anecdotal evidence that the selection process had an element of exclusiveness. Yet against that must be set Sister Mary Edith's impassioned plea to the Bishop of Wakefield that it was vital to offer a good Christian education to professional women, and to the wives and mothers of the future. This period was actually, or must have appeared to be, growing more godless than the rigidly pious society of the Victorian middle classes, into which the older Sisters had been born. These were the twenties, the years after the devastation of the First World War, when middle class society was often brittle and thoughtless, and the Sisters saw a need to set a standard.

A new school hall was built, since there was no longer room for everyone in the entrance hall to the Castle. In 1925 there was measles – too many cases for the new sanatorium. It is easy now, in the days of immunization, to forget the dangers of such epidemics, and the speed with which they could spread in enclosed communities.

The farm, intended to supply the Priory and school, as well as to make a profit, was acquired in 1925, together with various cottages and with them a number of legal problems which greatly exercised the community. A series of diaries and day-books, with considerable periods of time missing, discuss the misgivings of the community at these times. There was also concern about the spirituality of the community; whether the sisters were becoming too worldly; mixing too much with 'seculars'; going to every school event whether they were involved or not; eating too well; using condiments at every meal! The Order was 'up and running', but it still felt a need for inward contemplation to establish its final ethos, and it was struggling with Mother Margaret's concept of asceticism. In fact it was not until the end of this decade, in 1930, that the Rule was finally agreed and the legal Constitution drawn up. The latter was done with the aid of Fr Lucius Carey of the Cowley Fathers, a brilliant canon lawyer, who had, twenty years before, discussed with the 21-year-old Margaret Cope her wish to teach in the mission field.

In the midst of all their anxieties, there was, of course, the daily round of religious observance to be followed; the seven-fold Office of the *horarium*, the daily Mass, the calendar of saints and festivals to be kept. Special days of prayer had to be slotted in, together with confession, retreats or quiet days, both for the community as a whole, and often for the school. Then there was recreation, about which religious orders were very careful, allotting time daily for conversation and pursuit of personal interests and hobbies. It is small wonder that in the mid 1920s Mother Margaret was unwell with severe headaches and in desperate need of a rest.

Things were not improved for her by a farming depression and the general strike; by a growing reluctance of the pupils to observe all the religious duties, and by trouble with

> ### The Horarium
>
> *Religious life is very structured, and each Community establishes its timetable, or Horarium, with which every member of the Community must comply, unless given a dispensation for a special occasion or particular circumstances.*
>
> *From the Foundation until 1969, the Horarium of the Order was as follows:*
>
> | Time | Event |
> |---|---|
> | 5.40 am | Rise |
> | 6.15 am | Lauds and Prime |
> | 7.15 am | Mass |
> | 8.00 am | Breakfast |
> | | Housework |
> | 9.25-10.15 am | Terce and Quiet time |
> | | Work until |
> | 12 noon | Sext |
> | 1 pm | Dinner |
> | | Work |
> | 3 pm | None |
> | | Work |
> | 4.00-5 pm | Tea and Recreation |
> | 6 pm | Vespers |
> | 7 pm | Supper |
> | | Work |
> | 9 pm | Compline and then to bed |

lackadaisical prefects and difficult secular staff. *And* the school kept losing at hockey, which must have seemed almost a welcome anti-climax!

The accounts make it clear that money was always tightly balanced. The Order, struggling to pay off its mortgage and loans for improvements to the building, often had an overdraft despite careful book-keeping. School fees and donations were the principal income, though when sisters taught in church schools, they were paid a salary, which went into the community funds.

The sisters were concerned about a failure to attract new postulants to the Order, though perhaps, had they had the benefit of Susan Mumm's exhaustive study, they might have felt less despondent. There were by now far more opportunities for clever, energetic women to work at professions, to study – and take degrees – at university, and to travel overseas, than there had been in the heyday of the growth of the Victorian Sisterhoods. Moreover the Order had come to a town where women's opportunities had always been greater than normal.

And yet the Order survived, and grew both in size and in scope. The numbers of sisters and pupils had far outstripped the accommodation in the Castle itself, and at last building began on the Priory proper.

The accounts record the acquisition of a car, an Austin, bought for £245 in the financial year 1929-30. This must have made life much easier, since Scarborough is 21 miles, and York, albeit then still accessible by train (change at Malton) is 46 miles; it was cheaper for a single sister to go by public transport, but for more than one, it was certainly quicker and possibly cheaper by car. There was still the pony and trap, and a horse and rulley was used for transporting items around the buildings and pupils' luggage to and from the station.

A Love Affair with Africa

Thus does one of the sisters describe the Order's involvement with Africa, which began in 1925, and still continues. Yet it was a love affair which began by accident. The Chapter decision of 1919 had been made on the basis of a likely need within the Anglo-Indian community in the sub-continent, but as with Mother Margaret's ambition to work in India 15 years before, it was a different call that came.

A call to work as a missionary or in a professional capacity in the Third World, as well as to life as a member of a religious order, runs as a common thread through some sisters' lives. Indeed, Mother Margaret had herself explored the idea of mission teaching first. Sisters wrote: 'From my teens until College days, I had a secret ambition – to teach little Indian children under shady trees about Jesus…' and 'I was a missionary nurse in the tropics, apparently set for life… ' and 'I spoke to [Sr Rosa] about working in African agriculture'.

John Aglionby, one time Bishop of Accra, was instrumental in getting the sisters to go to the Gold Coast. In later years he wrote: 'Many are living transformed and happy lives, and all unknown to them, it is because one day the sisters came to West Africa.' The Bishop's words were echoed in 1971 by C K Graham, in *The History of Education in Ghana* who wrote of the influence of Christian education in the lives of women and their families and suggests that in the Gold Coast (unlike many other African societies), girls' education from the very beginnings of the educational process, was regarded as important.

Mary Wilkinson, the observant child at the start of OHP, recorded in one of her archived letters, of 1926,

Bishop John Aglionby

> 'We had a further link with OHP when, from St John's, The Brook, Liverpool, we saw the first contingent off to the Gold Coast. Also, when Sr Dorothy had to return very soon after, because of blackwater fever, I met her at Pierhead in December. Nothing remarkable about that except that a ship had spilt petrol in the Mersey that week and in biting cold weather all kinds of heating had to be abandoned because of the fire risk, so it was a very chilly welcome for her, to say nothing of the agony of waiting on the landing stage for hours.'

That brief account encapsulates the difficulties which the sisters faced, following Bishop Algionby's call to the 'white man's grave' that was the Gold Coast. Mother Margaret went with them and after a long voyage, in which they had to maintain the daily routine of convent life, they arrived off Cape Coast. The great terror was the mosquito-borne yellow fever, for which there was then neither immunisation nor cure. Yet if Sr Dorothy was sent home so quickly then she had clearly contracted malaria, of which blackwater fever is an advanced form.

Acquah's Hotel, Cape Coast, school premises 1926-31

One sister, speaking in 1977 of the early days in the Gold Coast, described a conversation at Mass in a local church on their first morning. The sisters asked why there was all this 'palaver' about boots, quinine, helmets and so on, when the Roman Catholic sisters did not have these. The reply was succinct; 'Have you yet seen their cemetery?' In fact, the only sister from the Order of the Holy Paraclete who died in Africa, succumbed in South Africa to a heart attack when in her 70s. The warnings about quinine and garments had been

Early days: the road from Cape Coast to Kumasi, en route to Mampong

heeded. It must have been very daunting at first, coping with an unfamiliar culture, with strange languages, with a fearsomely different climate from that of the north-east coast of England, although at Cape Coast they must at least have felt that there was the sea and, as when Sr Dorothy was shipped home, there was the chance of relief.

Their first House was in Acquah's Hotel, a former haunt of gold-prospectors and soldiers. It was in a crowded, noisy slum area, the roof leaked badly and the food supply depended on a very erratic market. There was nowhere to teach domestic science; it was far from ideal, but there they stayed for five years, and soon they had a convent and a primary boarding school for African girls established. And thus began the long service in Africa. In 1929 the sisters were asked to start teacher training, of which of course, they had experience.

They were also asked to move into the 'bush' in the Ashanti area. Here there was a different tribal group, with a different language. There, in 1930, they opened a convent dedicated to St Monica, and a new boarding school, with such luxuries as playing fields and space, unheard-of in crowded, urban Cape Coast. The senior girls transferred there, in some trepidation, for these were city girls, very anxious about moving into the 'bush' and quite certain there would be no food there!

Later, in 1936, the school in Cape Coast moved to better premises there, away from the sixteen roof leaks and the slums surrounding Acquah's Hotel. The training college moved north to Mampong, and the period of teacher training was increased from two to three years, and in 1937 the government was at last persuaded by the Bishop to open a girls' school in Accra, to match a well-established boys' school. The sisters took over the girls' school. Some time later, after the Second World War, a secondary school was set up in Mampong, and developed up to Sixth Form level during the 1950s. In all, Mother Margaret visited the Gold Coast eight times, prodding government officials into action.

The Journey to Mampong

The move to Mampong was not helped by old tribal rivalries between the Fante from the coast, and the Ashanti who lived round Mampong. The pupils from Cape Coast, on their way to the dreaded bush, were found to have smuggled live crabs with them, since it was manifest to them that there would be absolutely nothing edible in such wild territory. The crabs' box fell off the lorry, in the dark, on a dirt road, and the poor panicking creatures had to be rounded up and re-imprisoned by torchlight.

Meanwhile...

Other branch houses opened in England. Newcastle closed in 1932, releasing sisters for other work. This has been the pattern throughout. The Order responds to the depth of need, and at times hard decisions have to be made. In 1933 the Order opened a house in Leigh, in Lancashire, to work for three years in a secondary school. This would have been funded, as was all their teaching in state or church schools, with teachers' salaries paid to the Order.

In 1934 sisters began to work in the York Diocesan Retreat House in Hessle, outside Hull. They were to remain in the area for some forty years, with a twelve year gap. Two years later they were asked to go to Bugthorpe, a village near Stamford Bridge, where two sisters taught in the school until 1944. Meanwhile, a lull in the work at Whitby allowed Mother Margaret to visit the Holy Land in 1937, a visit which was to inform her teaching for many years.

In the Holy Land, 1937

Epilogue to Peace

But Armageddon threatened, and the Order which was born in wartime found itself once more in a restricted coastal area as war broke out again. It was to make communications with Africa difficult, though the Order continued its work in the Gold Coast, despite the hazards of U-boats. One sister's ship was torpedoed, but she escaped with her life, though without her profession candle and her cross, seeming to the Prioress to outweigh the saving of her life!

The school continued, with increasing restriction, until, on June 16th, 1940, news came of the fall of France. It is impossible now to describe the sense of urgency that beset the Order in Whitby. It is best conveyed in the words of the unknown sister who kept the day-book *(see Appendix II)*, clearly made up last thing at night, as the great exodus was arranged, to take the children away from the risk of occupation to safety in Canada.

One cannot but admire the Herculean labours of the Order to ensure the safety of their charges. Thereafter the daily frights and anxieties about the money in Canada, and about bombs being dropped on Whitby, as well as learning to live with their new neighbours, occupied the remaining sisters. They could visit those evacuated to Wemmergill but those in Canada were beyond reach except through official channels. Sr Ethel Mary, in her book *Fulfilled in Joy*, with justification describes this period as 'The Divided Years'.

Castle from West, 1915

Castle in 1920 – virtually as it was in 1915

Priory: first phase extension, 1929

A Brief History of SNEATON CASTLE

Over the years the Castle has seen a good deal of development since Colonel Wilson initiated alterations to the property in the 1820s.

When the Sisters came in 1915 they continued the business of adapting the buildings to suit new purposes. This is a brief chronicle of some of the changes which the Castle has been through.

CLAREMONT LODGE NEAR WHITBY

Classical and Commercial Seminary

A limited number of young Gentlemen are received as pupils

J. T. HOLLOWAY, D.D.

Late Fellow of Exeter College, Oxford, and a well-qualified Assistant from the South, and are instructed in the Greek and Latin Classics, Ancient and Modern History, Geography and the use of Globes, Writing and Arithmetic, Algebra & Mathematics, on the following Terms:

BOARD & INSTRUCTION,   **40 GUINEAS** per annum
ENTRANCE   **3 GUINEAS**

Extra charges for the Modern Languages, Drawing, Music and Washing. Each young Gentleman is requested to provide himself with a Silver Spoon and six Towels

NB THERE ARE GOOD ACCOMMODATIONS FOR SEA BATHING

As the number of pupils in this seminary is limited, one Quarter's notice or salary is required before the removal of a Pupil.

The house at High Stakesby, on the outskirts of Whitby, which later became Sneaton Castle was initially built, around 1813, by Revd Dr Holloway, late Fellow of Exeter College, Oxford as he liked to be styled. The new building, called Claremont Lodge, was to accommodate the expansion of the school which he had recently begun. The prospectus for the school is shown above.

Dr Holloway was also the priest at the New Chapel, a proprietary Anglican chapel which had been put up in Baxtergate in 1778 to provide a chapel of ease for the lower part of town. It appears that William Scoresby Junior, of the great whaling family, was much influenced by Dr Holloway and, perhaps in part due to this influence William became a clergyman.

Dr Holloway is described by Smales in *Whitby Authors* as 'one of the most distinguished Ministers that ever occupied our Whitby pulpits.' There is extant a copy of the sermon he preached on 11th January 1818, "occasioned by the lamented death of her royal Highness the Princess Charlotte Augusta of Wales." Reading it one is left with a distinct admiration for the powers of concentration of the congregation!

Dr Holloway built what is effectively the centre part of the facade of the present structure. Sadly, the deep depression which followed the end of the long Napoleonic wars caused the collapse of Whitby's shipping industry and Dr Holloway's plans for expansion of the school became untenable. He departed for the south in 1819, leaving Claremont and his ambitions behind him.

James Wilson

Just at that time, the Scots-born Colonel James Wilson came home from St Vincent in the West Indies where he had practised as a surgeon and had also been a member of the island's Governing Council. In 1815 the then Governor, John Lowry, had given Wilson a sugar plantation in recognition of his services. The plantation was worked by slaves – a list of them is still extant. Wilson had married Margaret Ann Falside in 1806 or 1807 and they had four daughters. Presumably Mrs Wilson died sometime between 1813 when her fourth daughter was born, and 1819 when James Wilson returned to Britain.

Clearly James Wilson was now a man of considerable means since he bought a large estate in the village of Sneaton as well as the tract of land at High Stakesby and Claremont Lodge.

Dr Holloway was fortunate to be able to sell the property at a good price. The receipt for the second of two instalments is extant – a sum of one thousand pounds (a great deal of money at that time).

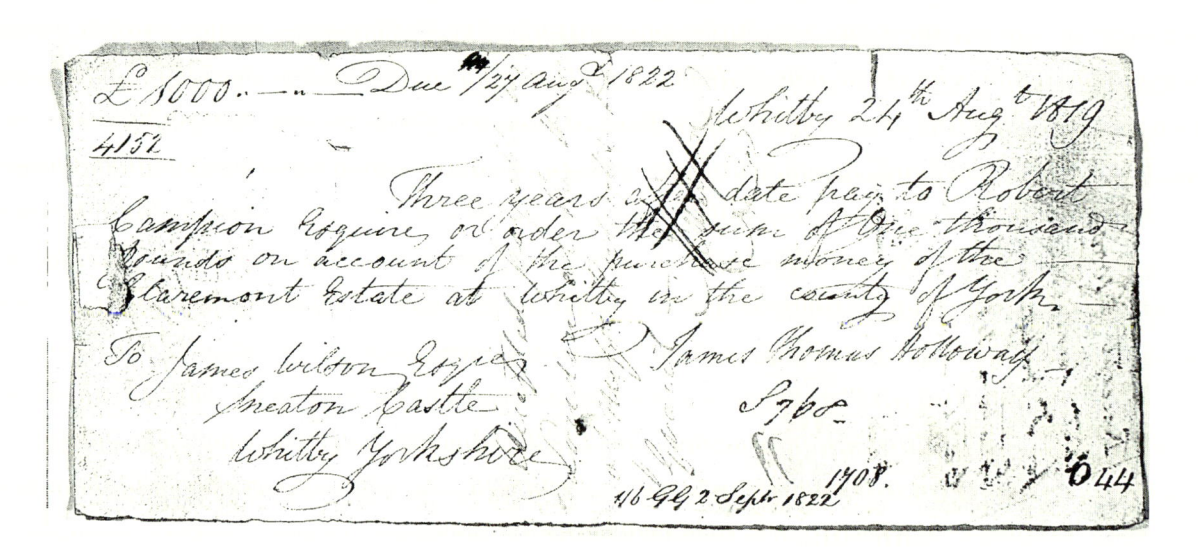

Colonel Wilson engaged the services of an architect, Mr Hurst, to convert the Lodge into a castle which was to resemble the ancient castle at Sneaton. This castle was no longer in existence but there was an old woodcut picture of it. Thus instructed Mr Hurst set to work adding two towers, one at each end of the original building. A castellated parapet was made and a wall built to enclose the garden. There was a fine carriage drive, stables, piggeries, outbuildings and staff quarters. In this splendour Wilson resided with his four daughters and their paid companions.

Mr Hurst was also commissioned to design a church and school building for the village of Sneaton. In order to travel easily between his village estate and the Castle Colonel Wilson had a bridge built across the Esk at Ruswarp.

WILSON OF SNEATON

SNEATON CASTLE, THE SEAT OF COLONEL WILSON, M.P.
In the North Riding of Yorkshire.

Wilson had obtained a patent for a coat of arms and this was carved in stone above the main entrance where it can still be seen. He must have been proud of his wealth for the coat of arms incorporates money bars in addition to the mullets used by other Wilson families.

Nevertheless he seems to have been a public-spirited gentleman and in 1826 became a Member of Parliament; we know that he was concerned about a new road to join Whitby to Lockton and promoted this amenity by "his best exertions" at Westminster.

Perhaps he contemplated a second marriage and the birth of a son for he went to considerable lengths to entail his fortune for the male line. But this was not to be. In 1830, four years after his election to Parliament, and being only in his early fifties, he died in London.

The estate went into trusteeship for the daughters. Nor was it as prosperous as had seemed for the property was heavily mortgaged. One of the daughters did not marry two married and produced only daughters, but Mary married James Richardson and had three sons and a daughter.

The *Whitby Gazette* of September 20, 1872, carried a notice of the timely appearance of a son and heir, James Wilson Richardson. The story of the Castle is not clear for the greater part of the nineteenth century; the property was leased to various people and seldom occupied by a member of the family.

When Mary Richardson (neé Wilson) died in 1907, her eldest son, Colonel Richardson, disentailed and sold the

> SNEATON CASTLE, NEAR WHITBY. —The heir of Sneaton Castle, in the township of Ruswarp, near Whitby, reached his majority a few days ago. His grandfather, by will, allotted 21 years for the birth of a son (the *first* male issue of any of his three married daughters) to inherit it, otherwise the castle was to be sold; but this young gentleman was born some 24 hours before that period was expired, and was therefore in time for the inheritance.
> —*Correspondent.*

In 1901 the premises were used as a preparatory school for boys by a Mr Bourne; the Whitby Gazette carried a notice of this in September 1903.

SNEATON CASTLE SCHOOL,
WHITBY.

PREPARATORY FOR THE PUBLIC SCHOOLS, AND THE ROYAL NAVY
UNDER THE NEW REGULATIONS.

Head Master, J. G. Bourne, B.A.

properties – both the Castle and the land in Sneaton village – to a Mr Brooksbank but this did not affect Mr Bourne's lease. The school continued until 1912 when Mr Bourne relinquished his lease to a Mr Charles Edwards who had intended to retain the school. However, at the outbreak of war in 1914 Mr Edwards took a commission in the Army and went overseas. Not long after he was wounded and invalided home, choosing to go to property he had in the south. So it was Mrs Edwards who negotiated the sub-letting to Margaret Cope, the future Foundress, and her companions. To judge from the inventories made at the time, Mrs Edwards took with her all that could be moved and the new occupants were faced with a rather daunting prospect of setting up the school and convent in a cold bare building in January! For the next 82 years the Castle was to house the Order's school.

The Castle had not really changed since Mr Hurst had made the extensions for Colonel Wilson but it now entered a new phase of development – which hardly seems to have ceased since the sisters came! In 1923 the Order managed to buy the Castle and the surrounding land (taking a mortgage to do so). Now the sisters could plan extensions and alterations to a property which they owned and this must have been a great relief, although money was still an anxiety.

The first concern was to provide adequate accommodation for the school and this was done by converting some of the outhouses to form the block now known as St Aidan's.

Constructing the archway, 1935

The school hall was built in 1924 with a dormitory above; this is now St Bede's. Shortly afterwards, in 1928, there was need for more space for the sisters and the first part of the Priory was built to be completed with a second phase in 1934.

The very first Chapel had been a room at the top of the South tower but that quickly became much too cramped and in 1919 a new, dignified, building was added (now forming the impressive centre refectory) and decorated with some striking paintings by John Duncan. When the present Chapel was opened in 1957 the vacated room was used as the school refectory and the paintings were left in situ. Gradually they deteriorated but happily in 1999 they were removed and restored and now hang on the main staircase of the Castle.

The Order and School celebrated their golden jubilee in 1965 and to mark the occasion the building now called St Cuthbert was erected, comprising two laboratories classrooms and sixth form accommodation. Originally the laboratory was housed in the present St Hilda Room but in 1967 this was altered and extended (to its present size) to become an art room.

Further needs in the Priory led to the construction of the library wing in 1954 and a new refectory in 1970. The Infirmary went up in 1975 but in response to need it was extended and remodelled in 1989.

One of the first photographs taken of the Chapel, 1925

Sadly, the Order had to close its school in 1997 but the buildings have definitely taken on a new lease of life as the Sneaton Castle Centre.

The most important building of all was, of course, the Chapel; designed by CD Taylor and completed in 1957 it has continued to meet the varying needs of the community, school and centre. Quite extensive refurbishing of the sanctuary was undertaken from 1992 and 2000 to a design produced by Ronald Sims.

One wonders what Dr Holloway and Colonel Wilson would make of all these changes and the activities which now take place at Sneaton Castle. We like to think that they would approve!

Sister Anita, OHP

Chapel and Castle at night, 1999

Castle and associated buildings

a	Original building	1813		j	St Aidan *dormitory block*	1919
b	Hurst's towers	1823		k	St Bede *school hall*	1924
c	Priory 1st phase	1928		l	Archway to quad *school library above*	1935
d	Priory 2nd phase	1934		m	St Cuthbert *laboratories & classrooms celebrating the Jubilee*	1965
e	Chapel	1957				
f	Library wing	1954		n	St Hilda Room *laboratory/art room*	1948/67
g	Priory refectory	1970				
h	Infirmary	1975 & 1989		o	Refectory *originally Chapel*	1919/58

Beyond the walled garden lie St Francis House, 1919, completely remade in 2000, and the Margaret Cope Centre, built to mark the Foundress's centenary in 1986. This Centre originally comprised music and computer facilities but has now been converted to an excellent conference auditorium and associated rooms.

Chapter 3   1940 – 1960

Between two watersheds

The two decades between 1940 and 1960 are marked for the Order by two watersheds, one being the disruption and upheaval of the evacuation of the school, followed closely by the death of the Order's oldest foundation member, Sr Mary Edith, early in 1941. The period ended with the results of the dramatic changes in the Order's principal field of work in Africa, and at home with the dramatic death of the Foundress, Mother Margaret in 1961.

The Second World War

To the Order, brought into being in the Great War, as to all those who had endured that conflict, World War II must have been a wearisome prospect. It brought specifically to OHP a long period of anxiety and change. The school was gone, although some temporary provision for day-pupils from the Whitby area was made, presumably for children whose parents did not wish them to attend school in the more vulnerable town. Life at the Castle among the remaining sisters was very much quieter, and this quietness, and probably increasing introspection by Mother Margaret, would inevitably have led to their having a less obvious rôle outside the Priory itself. Indeed, Old Girls noticed when they returned from Canada, that they saw less of those sisters who were not part of the school. Contact with the sisters in the Gold Coast was clearly much less frequent, because of risks to mail and the difficulty of sea travel.

> **State of the Order in 1940**
>
> *Mother Margaret was Prioress and Sr Mary Edith Sub-Prioress. There were 34 sisters in profession and several novices. There had as yet been no deaths and no sister had left the Order.*

There was, of course, the military occupation of part of the grounds, but that would have had little to do with the Priory itself, except in the use of the Chapel for church parades. A wartime novice wryly remembered spending hours polishing the chapel floor on Saturday and the soldiers trooping in on Sunday in their boots.

War brought a different kind of work to the sisters. Already involved at the diocesan retreat house at Hessle, they were asked by Archbishop Temple to help in Hull's worst-hit areas during the blitz, and went gladly to an onerous task. Hull's devastation was largely hidden by press references to 'a northern seaport', assumed by most readers to refer to

The Whitby Sisters   1940 – 1960

Mother Margaret and Miss Garbett on a visit to the Gold Coast in 1947

Newcastle-upon-Tyne, but the city suffered very badly indeed. One sister, later Assistant Chaplain at the University of Hull, recalls being accosted in the city by an elderly lady who remembered the sisters' great kindness and devotion during Hull's appalling ordeal.

The Order had never lost its link with Rievaulx, and in 1942 took over the all-age village school. That eventually closed, as educational reforms after the war set up new secondary schools, but there is still a branch house in Rievaulx.

War brought dangers to the Priory itself, first of all in 1940 in the shape of a German fighter plane shot down at Bannial Flatt, a short distance away. Then in 1942 incendiary bombs were dropped, and the Chapel received a direct hit, with one incendiary bomb coming straight through the roof.

In 1942 Cyril Garbett, Bishop of Winchester, became Archbishop of York in succession to Archbishop William Temple. He had been a socially aware Bishop of Southwark, with some of the worst slums of London in his care. He agreed to be the Visitor to the Order and he and his sister became close personal friends of Mother Margaret. He made his first Visitation of the Order the day after the incendiary fell in the Chapel, damaging the much admired Duncan frescoes *(see section on Sneaton Castle)*. When he died in 1955, Mother Margaret wrote a memoir with the simple title *Archbishop Garbett*.

But the hardest blow of all was not due to the war; on 6th January, 1941, Sister Mary Edith, who had endured so much in leaving Horbury to follow her vocation as a teaching sister, and who had been, as Sub-Prioress, an immense support and effective counter-balance to Mother Margaret, died aged 63, after a long and excruciating illness. She was much missed; she had been a strict, almost severe, disciplinarian but she had always been level-headed and fair. Her passing led to a growing remoteness in Mother Margaret. Entries in her sporadically-kept diaries, which were mainly used for teaching and

Sister Mary Edith

preaching notes, show brief glimpses of her grief, and a hint of the great value of her friendship with Mary Edith, to whom she could talk freely, and confidentially.

Sister Mary Edith's death also removed the only member who had experience of another Order. Mother Margaret took a long time before she replaced Sr Mary Edith as Sub-Prioress, by appointing Sr Anne, then Novice Mistress. The number of sisters left behind at the Priory was small during the war, sometimes even outnumbered by novices. Wartime life was austere anyway, so the additional austerity imposed by Mother Margaret must have seemed hard. With no resident pupils in the school, a sister professed in 1941 remembers that all the farm milk was sent to Whitby for the children there, so the novices clubbed together and bought two goats to provide milk, and later kids, which supplemented the meat ration. Fire-watching, gathering nettles and hedgerow fruit to supplement food, all took time, and had to be fitted round the Office and other duties. The duties of prayer were intensified during this period, probably under the influence of the Community of the Resurrection at Mirfield, and without Sr Mary Edith's restraining influence were, perhaps, excessive.

During this time Mother Margaret's sister Gwen and her husband, Gerald, moved away. A poignant and rare personal entry in Mother Margaret's diary records their last Sunday at Yarm, and a day spent at Goathland before they parted. Small wonder that Mother Margaret seemed to the sisters withdrawn. At a Retreat in 1942 she had confessed to being 'overwhelmed with busy-ness'. That sense of 'overwhelmedness' can only have increased in 1943.

At length, by 1944, it was decided that it was safe to bring some girls back from over-crowded and growing Wemmergill. The departing army had left behind at the Castle a large Nissen hut which had been a sick-bay, and the growing day-school took that over. (It later became the community laundry.)

A much later picture of Gwen & Gerald Healey, taken shortly before her death in 1962

Fortunately Carr Hall, on the river road from Sleights to Whitby, had become available, and the Order purchased it and its farm with the help of a mortgage. At the end of the year the Canadian contingent returned and most went to Carr Hall, though those who had grown during four years into seniors, went to the Castle. By July 1945, the day-school had been closed, the wartime need having gone, but there was still no real room for juniors. Wemmergill was given up in 1946 and the juniors had the temporary use of Fairhaven, adjacent to Carr Hall and Eggleston Hall near Middleton-in-Teesdale. A timely conditional deed of gift in 1947 made Hickleton Hall, owned by the Halifax family, available as a junior boarding school until it was returned to the family when Woodlands was bought in 1960.

The Whitby Sisters   1940 – 1960

Previous owners of Carr Hall had been very keen gardeners and tree-collectors; the house is set in impressive grounds

Hickleton Hall, near Doncaster, former home of Lord Halifax

Woodlands House

Vocations

Up to 1941, thirty-four sisters had made their Life Profession since the founder members had made theirs in 1921. There had been times when the Order had felt deep anxiety about the lack of new vocations, yet the sisters had achieved a great deal given their small numbers. They had set up and organised eight branch houses, three of them in the difficult conditions of the Gold Coast. They had built their Priory, and seen the school grow in size and reputation; they had coped with the great difficulties of evacuating the pupils to Erindale and Armadale in Canada and to Wemmergill, and they had withstood military occupation at the Castle and enemy action in Whitby, Hull and at sea. They had grieved for Old Girls killed on duty in the London blitz, and Mother Margaret had lost her brother, killed in the fall of Singapore.

During the war, ten more sisters made their Life Professions, and in the years to the end of the decade, a further fourteen, so that by 1950 the Order was much stronger. It had also absorbed the Order of St Michael and All Angels (OSMAA), a small community of teaching nuns in Leigh-on-Sea, Essex, whose declining numbers were added to those of OHP in 1946, when OHP set up a branch house in order to teach in the OSMAA school at Leigh.

By the end of 1960, the Order had added a further forty-one sisters in Life Profession, and it was this strength of numbers which made possible their greatest range of activities. Between 1942, when they opened a branch house at Rievaulx, and 1960, when Woodlands

The Whitby Sisters 1940 – 1960

at Sleights was bought to serve as a junior school, the Order opened eighteen new houses, eleven of which were in Africa, in addition to the ones already open in the Gold Coast. The work at Hessle continued until 1949, when the Retreat House was closed, as being too far from the centre of the Diocese of York, to reopen in 1951 under the care of OHP, at Wydale Hall near Scarborough, where the Order ran it until 1974. *(See page opposite for a tabulated summary of houses.)*

Several sisters have written of their early years in the Order towards the end of this period, so that it is possible to have a sense of the importance and intensity of their vocations and some of the ways in which they came to the Order, and their sense of being at home here. Some had been pupils and/or teachers at the school, and indeed there is

State of the Order in 1960

Mother Margaret was the Prioress, elected for life, Sister Anne was Sub-Prioress.

There were 95 sisters in life profession, more than half of whom were stationed overseas, and 15 novices. There had by then been 6 deaths and 3 sisters had left the order since its foundation.

evidence that towards the end of Mother Margaret's life, perhaps as she became aware of the passage of time, and of a sense of urgency, considerable pressures were applied to women within her influence to test their vocations, and, once there, to keep going, not always successfully or happily.

But by the 1960s there was an urge for commitment in the air: Voluntary Service Overseas (VSO), began in 1958, and several sisters had that as their background; the Kennedy Peace Corps was founded in the early sixties. The disruption of the war and immediate post-war period had been left behind.

The dramatic changes in Africa, as a westernisation process already under way accelerated during the war, with calls for independence and freedom from colonial status following hard upon the end of the war, meant greater need in that continent, a need which the Order was prepared to meet. These changes also brought backlash, with the beginnings of apartheid; with the Bantu Education Act, which curtailed secondary education for the vast majority of the Bantu population of South Africa; with civil war and UDI in Rhodesia. Economic chaos often followed, with coup and counter-coup, and within that unstable mélange, the Order continued and expanded its work and drew more women to service.

HOUSES OF THE ORDER
dates of opening and closure

Opening	House	Closure
1924	Tonge Moor, Lancashire	1928
1926	Cape Coast, Gold Coast	1976
1929	Newcastle-upon-Tyne	1932
1930	Mampong, Gold Coast	1982 finally
1932	Leigh, Lancashire	1936
1934	Hessle, East Riding	1949
1936	Bugthorpe, North Yorks	1944
1937	Accra, Gold Coast	continuing
1940	Wemmergill, Teesdale	1946
1940	Erindale, Canada	1944
1940	Armadale, Canada	1944
1942	Rievaulx	continuing
1944	Carr Hall, nr Whitby	1997
1946	Leigh-on-sea, Essex	1972
1946	Eggleston, Teesdale	1947
1947	Hickleton Hall	1960
1948	Wydale Hall	1974
1950	Frickley	1965
1951	Grace Dieu, Transvaal	1958
1952	St Agnes, Rosettenville	1956
1953	Holy Cross, Middlesbrough	1957
1954	Maternity Hospital, Mampong	1972
1954	Penhalonga, Rhodesia	1978
1956	St Benedict's, Rosettenville	continuing
1958	Daramombe, Rhodesia	1971
1958	Marion Institute, Capetown	1969
1959	St Michael's, Manzini (teaching until 1984)	1997
1959	St Anne's Home, Capetown	1970
1959	Zonnebloem College, Capetown	1970
1960	St David's, Bonda	1979
1960	Woodlands, Sleights	1987
1962	St Chad's House, Hull	1977
1965	Bathlaros, South Africa	1967
1968	Thokoza, Mbabane	1974
1970	Rättvik, Sweden	1972
1970	Doughty St, London	1987
1976	Bolgatanga, Ghana	1989
1978	Bishopslea, Harare	1982
1979	SCH Dunblane	1994
1980	Kalmar, Sweden	1983
1980	Lancaster	1994
1980	Gt Gaddesden	1991
1982	Cranborne, Zimbabwe	1989
1983	St Oswald's, Sleights	continuing
1987	Beachcliff, Whitby	continuing
1987	Martin House Hospice	1999
1989	Lambeth Palace	1993
1991	St Michael's House, Leicester	2000
1996	St Hilda's House, Dundee	1999
1997	St Hilda's House, Manzini	continuing
2000	Jachie, Ghana	beginning
2000	Hull	continuing

The Whitby Sisters   1940 – 1960

Tertiary Order

One of the most interesting developments of the late 1940s was the foundation of the Tertiary Order of the Holy Paraclete. In 1946 Dr Charlotte Houlton, CBE, retired from medical work in India. An old university friend of Sr Ethel Mary, she had long been interested in the religious life and from her new home close to the Priory she envisaged an Order for secular persons. They would live a life which used an adaptation of the Rule, be supported spiritually by the Order, and would in turn support the Order's work. Their base was St Francis House, within the Castle grounds, to which non-resident Tertiaries came for retreats and annual Chapter meetings. A few became Tertiaries Regular and lived there, wearing a navy-blue habit, and working with the professed sisters, at home or overseas. The last of these died in 1995.

Charlotte Houlton. Founder of the Tertiary Order. The habit was blue and a belt was worn rather than a girdle

Consecration of the Chapel, 1957 (note the identification labels placed on original photograph)

After the death of Charlotte Houlton in 1956, the appointment of Tertiary Warden lay in the hands of the Prioress and several sisters have fulfilled that rôle, notably Sr Mary Nina, who acted as Warden for 26 years. The Tertiary Order is world-wide, and open to both men and women, from all walks of life, and of any Christian Trinitarian denomination.

Developments at the Priory

The growth in numbers of the Order meant a new need for expansion as building regulations eased after the war. A fund had long been in existence to build a permanent Chapel for the Priory and school and at last this was started, with plans produced by an architect parent who lived locally, Mr Charles Taylor. The foundation stone was laid in May, 1955, and the finished building was consecrated by the Archbishop of York, the Most Revd Michael Ramsay, in May 1957, to great rejoicing.

Work in England

Three new projects were undertaken in England, both in Yorkshire, before 1960. The sisters had been forced to withdraw from Bugthorpe in 1944 because of illness, though the school at Rievaulx continued till 1962. However, from Hickleton Hall they undertook the care of the village school, with one sister acting as Head, and continuing until 1962 after the Hall was returned to the Halifax family. In 1950 one sister became sole teacher at the school at Frickley, a colliery village near Doncaster, where the Order worked until 1965.

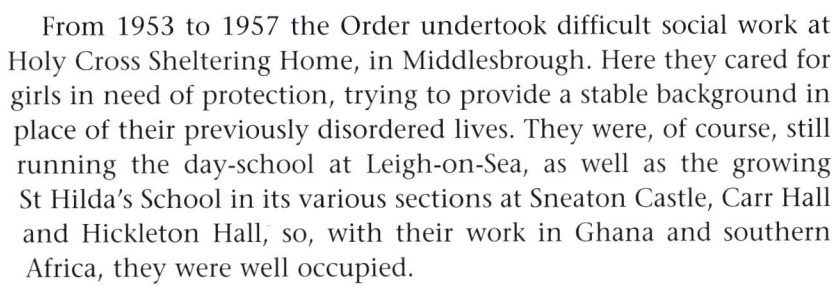

From 1953 to 1957 the Order undertook difficult social work at Holy Cross Sheltering Home, in Middlesbrough. Here they cared for girls in need of protection, trying to provide a stable background in place of their previously disordered lives. They were, of course, still running the day-school at Leigh-on-Sea, as well as the growing St Hilda's School in its various sections at Sneaton Castle, Carr Hall and Hickleton Hall, so, with their work in Ghana and southern Africa, they were well occupied.

When Woodlands Hall was bought it was possible to move the junior school from Hickleton Hall and so the full age range of St Hilda's School was re-established in the Whitby area.

In the early 1950s, the *Church Times* commissioned a series of articles on the religious life for women. Many of the articles were written by the novices, with individual sisters supplying the latter part of the story, and Mother Margaret co-ordinating the whole. They were eventually published as a book, *I Choose the Cloister*, in 1956, under the pseudonym of Rosemary Howard-Bennett, and provide a useful insight into the Order in the 1950s.

The Whitby Sisters   1940 – 1960

Sweden

During this period, Mother Margaret became very involved with the work of the World Council of Churches, and particularly with the Lutheran Church in Sweden. She paid several visits to the country, and conferences of clergy from both churches were held alternately in Whitby and Sweden. There had begun to develop in Sweden in the thirties a high church movement not unlike the Oxford Movement of the Anglican Church. This series of discussions was to continue into the seventies.

Sr Philippa with a group of student midwives

Continuing in Africa

Work in the Gold Coast Colony had been a tremendous challenge, to which the sisters had successfully risen, and which they had managed to maintain and indeed expand, during the long years of the war. Their only contact had been by mail, often disrupted, or by the dangerous transfer of sisters to and from the Gold Coast houses.

In 1945, and again in 1947, Mother Margaret made long tours of several months to West Africa. Between her two visits, the sisters had begun to take some medical work into the outlying rural communities, and in 1948 Sr Miriam went out as school matron, in charge of the dispensary. From that developed midwifery work and by 1954 a new government-requested maternity hospital had been opened, complete with training school for African midwives and Sr Philippa as midwifery tutor. In due course, at the request of the Mampong people, a home for motherless babies was opened and continues under a Ghanaian director.

Sr Bertha with Mother Margaret

In 1950 a most significant event took place when the first African sister made her profession. Not only was this a first for OHP, Sister Bertha was the first African to be professed in the Anglican Church. Mother Margaret went to Mampong for the ceremony.

The Gold Coast became the independent state of Ghana in 1957, with Dr Kwame Nkrumah as its first Prime Minister. Three years later it became a republic with Dr Nkrumah as its President. Slowly a process of Africanisation took place, and African teachers began to take over the teaching, and teacher training. The new political developments changed the perception of the Anglican Church in Ghana. It ceased to be a mission area and became a member church of the Anglican communion.

Farther into Africa

The next call to Africa came from South Africa. Until 1950 much of the mission teaching work there had been done by the Sisters of the Community of the Resurrection of Our Lord, a South African Community based in Grahamstown. They trained teachers at their mother house, and had other houses throughout South Africa and Southern Rhodesia. (They had no connection, other than their dedication, with the Community of the Resurrection at Mirfield.)

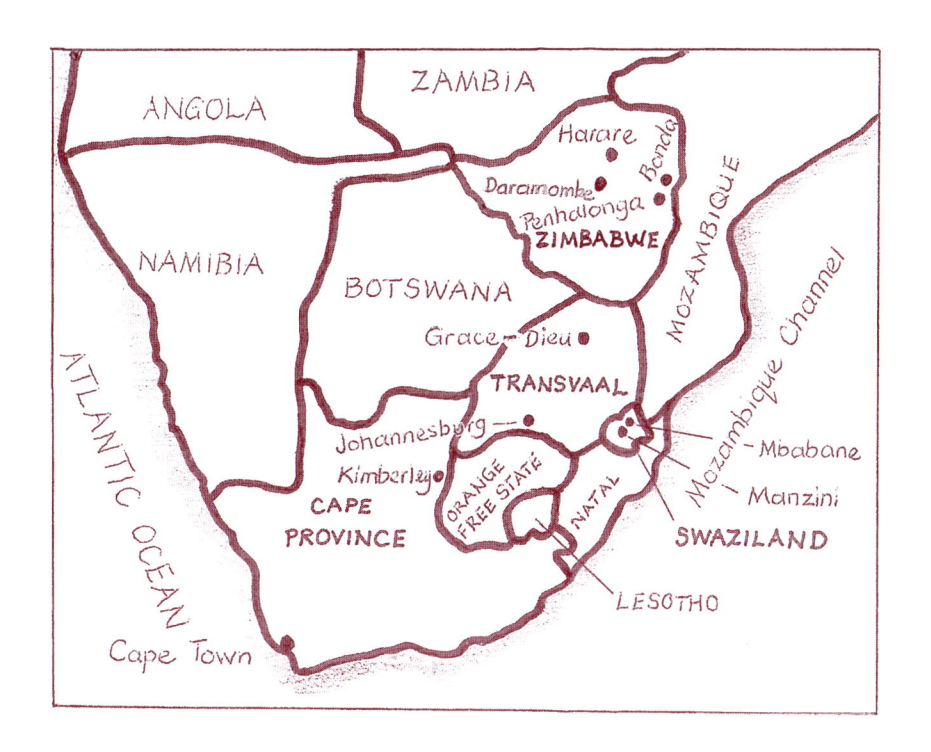

The Whitby Sisters   1940 – 1960

The CR Sisters were having to withdraw from many of their enterprises, and the Bishop of Pretoria invited OHP to consider taking over. A visit by Mother Margaret and the Sister Provincial from Ghana, in 1950, thinking that it was for only one 'piece of work', led to their acceptance of the invitation and, within ten years, to work in South Africa, Southern Rhodesia and Swaziland. The Community of the Resurrection from Mirfield, among whose members was Fr Trevor Huddleston, the great fighter against apartheid, was itself heavily involved in South Africa.

The list of branch houses shows an almost breathless urgency in the fifties. In 1951 four sisters went to Grace Dieu in the Transvaal to take over the teacher-training work of the Grahamstown Sisters. The sisters remained there until 1958 when the work was seriously affected by the notorious Bantu Education Act of 1955, which effectively banned the education of black pupils beyond the sixth grade (top of primary school).

The CR brethren ran St Peter's School in Rosettenville, Johannesburg, for black pupils, and three sisters went there to run St Agnes' Hostel for female pupils, and one taught in the school. In addition, another sister did parish work in Johannesburg among African women

Srs Rosa and Kathleen in Grace Dieu, Transvaal

Sr Madeleine teaching children at the TB clinic, Bonda

who worked as domestic servants. Again St Peter's fell foul of the Bantu Education Act, and of the Group Areas Act, which caused the CR fathers to close the school, as a protest against the impossibility of working with the South African government.

It was a demanding time. One sister writes of working in the Johannesburg area in the 1950s, and of the helplessness they felt when a mother appealed for assistance in keeping her two-year-old child Absalom with her, after she had been ordered to send him back to her family in the 'homelands'. One of the tasks the sisters undertook was to run Mothers' Union and Girls' Guild branches for African house-servants. One of them called one day to see a girl who had missed several Guild meetings, and found she had died in her room in the garden. No-one had bothered to look after her when she became ill.

There was much distress in the Order over the Bantu Education Act, and an angry Mother Margaret wanted the Order to continue its work at St Peter's School in Rosettenville when the CR fathers refused to work with the government. The sisters taught for the whole of their last year unsalaried, living on their savings, but the task proved impossible. In the end wiser counsels prevailed among OHP, and the work was reluctantly given up. The OHP sisters left St Peter's in 1956 but stayed in Rosettenville, where they were asked by the CR fathers to run St Benedict's Retreat House, opposite the theological college where Desmond Tutu trained. They are still there. From St Benedict's, pastoral work was done at the large Baragwanath Hospital in Soweto.

The Whitby Sisters   1940 – 1960

Dormitory Blocks, Bonda

(Below) Fr Sidebottom and Sr Lucy with St Christopher's Guild at St Peter's Church, 1960

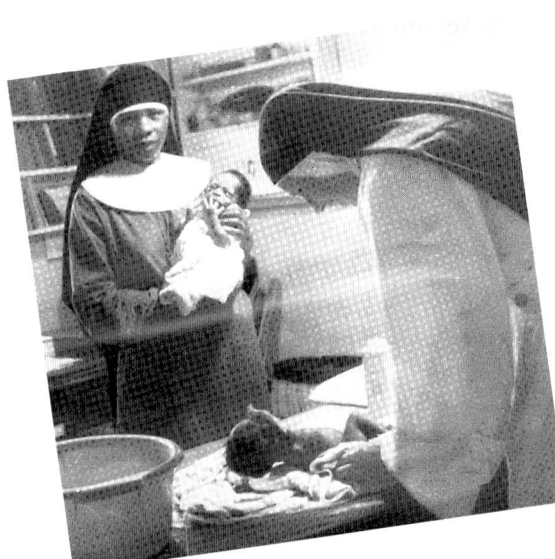

(Left) Sr Felicity and Sr Mary Catharine at the Clinic, Penhalonga

Laying the foundation stone for the new Chapel, 1967

Sr Elsa was by then Sister Provincial in Southern Africa and, when the feared Special Branch came to search the school for evidence of sedition, she successfully concealed the manuscript of *Naught for your Comfort*, Fr Huddleston's seminal book on apartheid, under her mattress.

In 1958, members of the Order went south to Capetown, to District 6, to become involved in several enterprises already established, including the Marion Institute, a base for social work among the Cape coloured community, and Zonnebloem College for teacher training for coloured students. They were also living and working at St Anne's Home, a mother and baby home. District 6 was so notorious that some of this must have been almost like a return to the *raison d'être* of some of the Victorian Anglican Sisterhoods.

Mother Margaret was asked to send sisters to Swaziland, to St Michael's School, in Manzini, a primary school for coloured children. Some pupils risked coming over the border from South Africa to obtain at St Michael's the kind of education that was not available to them in South Africa because of the restraints of the Bantu Education Act.

Swaziland was free of apartheid, being a British colony, having her own king, and governed by tribal custom. South Africa's request to take it over had been rejected by Britain in 1949, and at this stage it remained a colony. It was to achieve limited self-government as a British Protectorate in 1963, and in 1968 it became a fully independent constitutional monarchy within the Commonwealth.

Meanwhile in 1954, the CR fathers had also requested help from the Order with work in Southern Rhodesia. Sisters were asked to teach in the teachers' training college and secondary school at Penhalonga, and to care for the girl students in St Monica's Hostel. Four more sisters went in 1958 to the teachers' training college at Daramombe and in 1960 two sisters to St David's School, Bonda.

Throughout all this political turmoil, Mother Margaret had continued to travel between England and Africa and had been very involved in all the decisions, not always seeing eye-to-eye with the Sister Provincial over the best course of action!

The Second Watershed

It was just such a visit to Ghana which was planned for Mother Margaret in February, 1961. On Sunday, February 12th she went to Carr Hall to speak to the Middle School pupils in Chapel, and to say goodbye to the resident sisters. After Chapel, she was on her way to the sisters' community room on the first floor but preoccupied perhaps by a previous conversation, she turned too soon on the landing and fell down the back stairs, fracturing her skull; she lived for about five hours, not regaining consciousness. She was 74 years old, and in the 40th year of her Life Profession.

She was brought back to the Castle the next day and after cremation at Hartlepool, her ashes were buried under the altar in the Chapel. The Archbishop of York, Michael Ramsay, preached at her Requiem, and many spoke and wrote of her contribution to religious life and education. *Fulfilled in Joy*, written as a memorial, records the ceremonies of her burial.

Margaret Cope had led a remarkable life, and achieved and inspired an extraordinary amount of good. She had founded an Order which flourished, which did not flinch from the world's problems and which was prepared to go anywhere to serve. As an educationalist she was remarkably forward-looking and put many of her ideas into practice in St Hilda's School, the Order's foundation work, as well as in the wider world of education. She was an inspiring teacher; the Cambridge examiner who awarded her distinction in 1908 knew not what he had let loose on the world of education!

She was a deeply spiritual woman, to whose life the Blessed Sacrament was central, and whose devotion to prayer was at times overwhelming. She had risked much, been bold in her decision-making, and idealistically democratic in the construction of her institutions. She was a brilliant financial organiser, which was probably as well, given the risks she took, and the penury in which the Order started out.

As Cosmo Gordon Lang found when he tried to suggest her youth as a bar to her ambition, she was capable of a sharp answer. Former pupils vary between deep devotion to her memory and a certain reserve about some of her attitudes to modern living. Sisters who knew her also vary; there are those who found her either wholly good, or what she was, a remarkable woman with human flaws. Her diaries show her to have been well aware of her faults. But she had laid her foundations well and, after the shock of her death had been overcome, the Order went on to even greater strengths.

Chapter 4 The Sixties and Seventies

With the death of the Foundress of the Order, many changes were almost bound to take place, some of them deliberate, others simply as a result of her absence. Sister Anne, who had previously been Novice Mistress till she became Sub-Prioress after the death of Sr Mary Edith some twenty years before, was elected Prioress. Like most founding Prioresses, Mother Margaret had eventually been elected for life. Mother Anne was, however, elected for only five years, but her term of office was later extended for a further five, according to the Constitution.

There is anecdotal evidence that the Community of the Resurrection at Mirfield, which had worked with Mother Margaret on the spiritual side of the Order from the start, could not imagine how the Order would continue. It was wrong. The sisters were far too strong in their convictions and determination to continue in their chosen life for the Order to fade

Mother Anne, Prioress 1961-71

away. In fact, the change was positive. One older sister, writing of Mother Margaret, suggested that while she was brilliant with individuals, she was no organiser, and had no idea how to delegate. Others speak of a sense of shock at her death, but not a lasting grief. An Old Girl calling at the time was surprised at the extent of the returning joy. Whatever its cause, that joy drove all the sisters forward to tackle the new challenge.

There was another bereavement within two years, with the death in 1962, of Gwen Healey, Mother Margaret's younger sister. Fr Healey spent his remaining years at the Castle, in a bungalow attached to St Francis House, until he died in 1977. Both are buried in the Priory cemetery.

Vocations

Life Profession is the final commitment to the religious life, and from 1921 until 1966 novices normally proceeded straight to Life Profession. If after Life Profession a sister wished to leave, then her case was dealt with by the Chapter, and she could apply for exclaustration (a period of time outside the convent) to think through her decisions, or for dispensation from her vows, which could be granted only by the Visitor, the Archbishop of York.

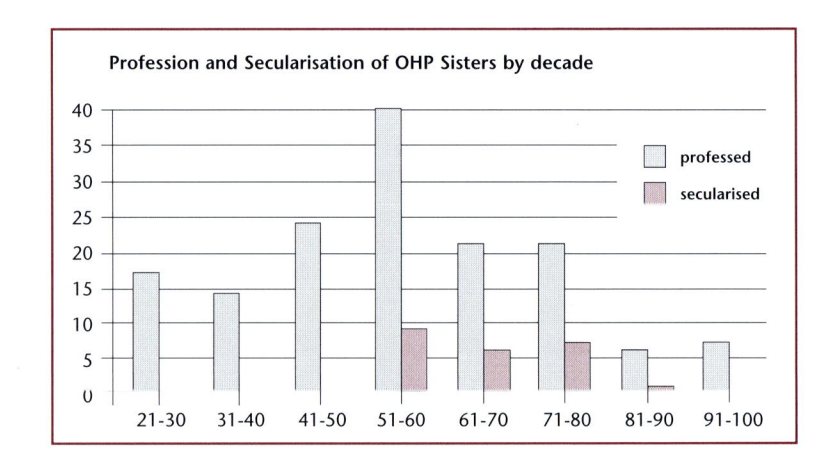

Profession and Secularisation of OHP Sisters by decade

It was in the decade 1951-60 that the Order had its largest number of new Life Professions. Forty sisters made their profession during these years, part of the generation which had grown up during the war, and had honed their social and spiritual consciences in the years afterwards. Yet it was also this cohort which produced the Order's first secularisations.

In the past women had come to the Order to test their vocations as postulants and novices. A few had been advised to leave as being unsuitable, and many other novices had eventually realised that this was not the life they sought. Life Profession, on the other hand, was a serious commitment, and the shock to the community of sisters actually leaving after taking their final vows must have been severe.

All of those who left had remained in profession for at least six years, so the decisions were not precipitate, while for nine sisters the break came after between sixteen and thirty years. Of the 'fifties' cohort 35% have been secularised. It may well be that some of those who left had been subjected to undue pressure by Mother Margaret in her last years, but of course, such large percentages cause alarm; what is equally true is that 65% of the cohort stayed.

During the next two decades, 1961-80, a further forty-two sisters made their Life Profession, of whom thirteen have been secularised, a percentage lowered a little by the fact that a major change was made to the Constitution in 1966, instituting the concept of First Profession, followed by Life Profession. Again the proportion of secularisations seemed high. However, in the context of contemporary change in the durability of marriage, or of other kinds of vocation such as professional careers – and the sisters concerned were mainly well-qualified professional women – then the rate probably reflects the times rather than any inherent dissatisfaction with the Order *per se*. Several of the present sisters, writing anonymously of their vocations, admit to wanting to give up in the face of adversity, or even to a shaking of their faith, but they have soldiered on and been glad they did.

Ghana

Of the thirteen new branch houses which had been opened between 1951 and 1960, ten continued into the next decade, and seven into the decade after that. In addition, seven of the earliest branch houses, in England and Ghana, were still open, and six of those carried on into the 1970s. Of the houses in Ghana, all except Accra had closed by 1980, although when a Ghanaian midwifery tutor was appointed to teach at Mampong, in 1978, one sister remained to assist her. The institutions that had been set up, however, continued under Ghanaian leadership. After Independence, and the changes in government brought about by the country's *coups d'état*, of which there were four between 1966 and 1979, the running of the schools and colleges was gradually handed on to the Ghanaian people, many of whom would have been trained by the Order in the first place. These institutions were by then fully funded by the Ghanaian government. It was, in fact, the accepted practice of the Order that this should happen.

However, in 1976, a new house was opened in Ghana, at Bolgatanga, in the north of the country, bordering the Sahel region. Three sisters began vocational training and evangelistic work there, and this work continued under the sisters until 1989, when it was handed on to the Ghanaian Church.

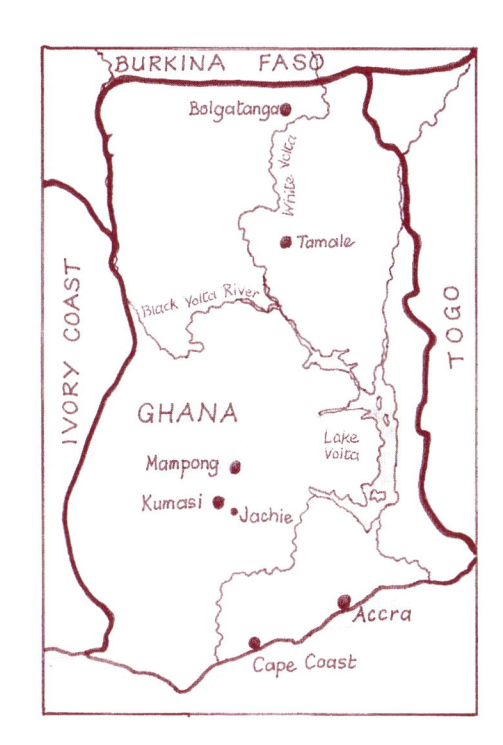

Continued on page 46

Bishop's palaver, near Bolgatanga, Northern Ghana

The Office of Prioress

The Foundress, Mother Margaret, was elected to the office of Prioress for life. The Order's Constitution provides for the election of the Prioress for a five-year term with the possibility of re-election for a further term after which she must stand down for five years. Mother Anne followed the Foundress; her time in office is described quite fully in Chapter 4. The present Prioress is Sister Judith.

Mother Marguerite
Prioress 1971-79
professed 18th December 1934
died 2nd July 1992

Marguerite Chapman was a teacher at St Hilda's School before she joined the Order in 1932; to the end of her days she rejoiced in the privilege of having read history at Oxford!

For the greater part of her life in community Marguerite worked in the school and was headmistress for more than twenty years. Generations of St Hilda's girls testify to the encouragement and inspiration she gave them and the loyalty and affection she inspired.

As Prioress she undertook the revision of the Order's documents – with tenacity and determination! She introduced weekly house meetings at the Priory and established the principle of dealing with community business by committee.

A dignified, disciplined, steadfast woman she was a perfectionist in all she did. In the community she was a kind of elder stateswoman whose counsel was greatly valued.

**Sister Janet
Prioress 1979-89
and 1994-98**

professed 15th June 1955

Janet Wishart had been a pupil in the school and was part of the evacuation to Canada; a well-qualified nurse she entered the Order in 1952 and made her profession in 1955.

She served as both Chauntress and Novice Mistress as well as working as school matron. Not being a teacher she could manage to take part in activities outside the Mother House and had already become quite well known in wider church circles before her election. As Prioress she was a founder member of the Communities Consultative Council and served on the Advisory Council. Her presence as a chaplain at the Lambeth Conference of 1998 was significant for the Order's image. Within the community she was responsible for initiating many practical changes – improved diet, adaptation of the habit (off with the wimple!) and revision of the Office. The Prioress was now called Sister not Mother. During her tenure various houses were set up: St Oswald's Pastoral Centre, Beachcliff and Martin House reflecting her concern for those in need of spiritual direction and special care.

She came back for a second term in 1994 and retrospectively was widely seen as the only person who could have handled the closure of St Hilda's School and its aftermath.

Alison Prince had a Social Science background and shortly after her profession she went out to Capetown to work in the famous District 6. On her return to England she pioneered the Order's work in York and later served as Novice Mistress.

As Prioress she had a wide-ranging pastoral role – ministering not only to the sisters but to their families and friends. In her desire to get the structures and procedures of administration right she brought in expert help – including the Archbishop and a retired university registrar.

The notion of "shared responsibility" in branch houses (in place of a Sister-in-charge) took root and flourished under her guidance as did that of conciliar support for the Prioress. But perhaps she influenced the community most by her personal standards of simplicity of life, her dedication, and her refreshing sense of wonder towards all created things.

**Sister Alison
Prioress 1989-94**

professed 2nd April 1957

Southern Africa

The South African houses that had closed before 1961 did so as a direct result of the Bantu Education Act. The new houses in Capetown's District 6, and in Manzini in Swaziland, had become the main focus of the Order's work in Southern Africa, alongside the work in Johannesburg.

Together with the work at Bolgatanga in Ghana, the South African houses represent the start of a change in the Order's way of working. Hitherto, apart from occasional parish work in England, all the Order's work had been institutional, but for the first time in Africa, houses were opened for **non-institutional** work. In these houses, sisters lived together, but each had her own individual ministry, apart from the community life of the house. Perhaps the most unusual diversification in Africa was among the sisters who from 1965-67 worked at the Mission hospital in Bathlaros in the north of Cape Province in South Africa. Three sisters went there, two to work in the hospital and one who, among other duties, ran the Post Office!

As District 6 was cleared and the inhabitants moved under the Group Areas Act, further changes happened to the sisters' work in South Africa. In 1966 they left Zonnebloem College, although they continued to work in the Marion Institute and St Anne's mother and baby home, which was badly needed in that area. When these duties were finally handed over in 1970, they moved to St Aidan's House, in Rosebank, becoming involved in a wide range of activities in Capetown, until 1978.

Life for the Anglican church in the apartheid years in South Africa was extremely difficult. Its open opposition to the pass laws, and to the worst manifestations of the régime, led to virtual persecution by the authorities. The sisters would see clergy colleagues thrown into prison, or put under house arrest, and their letters home were probably subject to interference, or may even have failed to turn up. They themselves dealt with the daily cruelties of the system, which forbad African house servants to have their families, even their small children, with them in the white areas.

It was a dreadful time, yet they soldiered on right through the repeal of apartheid to the release of Nelson Mandela and the change of government, and are still there, struggling with the country's economic problems, with the various local 'mafia' and with the high rate of violent crime. There is work to be done, and there are willing hands to do it.

The work begun in Swaziland, South Africa's neighbour, in 1959, and increased by the Bantu Education Act, developed further in the 1960s, with a new house, Thokoza Hostel for schoolgirls attending local secondary schools, in Mbabane. Thokoza was opened in 1968, a year after the first Zulu sister made her profession, and closed in 1974. The novitiate in Manzini, opened during the 1960s for African women, closed in 1970. However, work in St Michael's School continued to flourish. It was a time of cumulative development in both primary and high schools with Sr Prudence's work coming to fruition. Independence and stability made the involvement of the Swazi community in its own affairs much greater, and today over two-thirds of the population is literate, despite education being neither free nor compulsory. The University College of Swaziland was opened in 1964, and there are training colleges for teaching, agriculture and industry, so that the pupils who came out of St Michael's School no longer had to seek higher education in South Africa.

In the much larger Southern Rhodesia, the sisters' work at Penhalonga and Daramombe continued. In 1960 the sisters went to develop St David's, Bonda, the first all-girls secondary school for African pupils. This was in fact the only completely OHP undertaking of the three. As with many of the African colonies, by far the greatest part of educational work had been undertaken by the Missions.

At Daramombe the work had been in teacher training, and four sisters had worked there and in an attached school, where they remained until the early seventies. The Mission is in Mashonaland, at the centre of a vast tract of high veldt, about the size of Yorkshire, and when the sisters began their work, it was poor, and the people were undernourished. Daramombe lay at the centre, and covered all the outlying villages and settlements. One sister who worked there spoke highly of the community sense of the Shona people, and wrote that she loved the house above all the others she had worked in. She particularly enjoyed the teacher training because it was **enabling**, and because going out to see students on teaching practice gave her such an insight into life in the outlying communities.

In 1965, Ian Smith's right-wing party declared UDI for Southern Rhodesia, and sanctions were imposed by the UN. This led in time to the wars of independence, in which conflict among the Government forces, Robert Mugabe's Shona based ZANU and Joshua Nkomo's ZAPU organisations, caused huge disruption. In 1977 St David's School, at Bonda, with the five sisters, had to be hastily evacuated to Umtali, away from the war zone. The next year they also withdrew, on advice from the Shona staff, from Penhalonga. In the same year a secular head was appointed to St David's, and when the school returned to Bonda at the end of hostilities, before reluctantly-agreed elections were held in 1980, the sisters did not return with them. They had been asked in 1978 to become involved with Bishopslea, a Church school in Salisbury (now Harare), to increase the number of African pupils.

Sweden

Mother Margaret's long-standing involvement with the established Lutheran Church in Sweden led to lengthy discussions as to whether community life could be established in that church. Some Swedish novices were trained at the Priory, and founded small communities for women. The Lutheran Church has its own Order of Deaconesses, but had previously had no religious sisterhoods. OHP itself made two attempts to establish branch

Kalmar: Tvö Systras Kapell

houses in Sweden, the first of which was a short-lived venture in Rättvik, from 1970-72. A later house opened at Kalmar in 1980, lasting about three years, before that also closed. However, Sr Birgit, who had worked in Kalmar, remained a member of OHP.

Diversification in England

The same practice, of diversification of work within branch houses, rather than branch houses for a single institution, was developing more widely in England, with the opening of St Chad's House in Hull, in 1965, and of the London house in Doughty Street WC1, in 1970. Some of the impetus for these changes had come from the Roman Catholic Church, whose Vatican II conference of 1962-65 had encouraged their religious to go out into the community in a similar way. In Hull, for instance, one OHP sister acted as Head of St John's Newland Primary School, while others worked in the school, or in the University chaplaincy. A similar pattern emerged at the London house, from which one sister worked at Westminster Abbey, two Sisters taught at Clerkenwell Parochial School, and others undertook study or worked in the University chaplaincy. It was very much an experimental venture.

Sr Muriel and prefects, St John's School, Hull

Outside the Doughty Street house in London

Concomitant with these changes was a reduction in the number of sisters involved in teaching in St Hilda's School.

A house was opened in York in 1972, and two sisters moved there, to work in the Minster helping with the huge increase in visitors expected for the 500th anniversary of the Minster's completion. Initially they also undertook ecumenical work with other Orders in York, and in the Diocese. Then gradually they became involved with education, and with explaining the Minster to students and children, their work increasing as the number of school parties and field-trips grew, till the Minster Chapter created the post of Education Officer, held by successive sisters for twelve years. One sister acted as Warden of St William's College in Minster Yard, while others assisted in the Minster Library and at services. Sisters are a long-familiar sight in the Minster precincts, and the outreach from this work has brought at least one new member to the Order.

University chaplaincy work was undertaken, from 1965 in Hull, and later in York, Nottingham, London and Lancaster. The sister in York later became Secretary for women's ministry for the Diocese. A series of University of Hull Public Lectures at the University's Centre in Whitby, and the present use of the new Sneaton Castle Centre by the University for field study trips has renewed that particular link in the present day.

Another change in the Order's ways of working came with the vocation of one particular sister to healing, which led to the opening of a house at Cleadon, near Sunderland, where work was undertaken in Cleadon Healing Home. The house remained open from 1968-1971. At the same time, the work at Leigh-on-Sea, where the sisters had been called in during the 1940s to assist the declining Order of St Michael and All Angels (OSMAA), was handed over in 1971 to the local parish. The sisters also withdrew finally, in 1974, from running Wydale Hall as a diocesan retreat house. It was a kind of work they had been involved with since they first tackled the cockroaches of Hessle in 1934.

There were changes to the buildings at Whitby for both the sisters and the school during this period, particularly for the Golden Jubilee of the Order in 1965. The principal construction in honour of that event was the building of a complete new wing to house new school laboratories. The former laboratory, provided when the first chapel was built in 1919, became an Art Room. Later in 1970, a new refectory for the sisters was completed, and in 1975 there followed a new infirmary wing, built on to the library wing, in response to the needs of a community more of whose early members were growing old. The Order had by then been in existence for 60 years.

Come North!

There was already one venture into northern Europe, in Sweden, but the invitation from the Bishop of St Andrews to work at Scottish Churches House in Dunblane, with its thirteenth century Cathedral and in a country where the established church was Presbyterian was novel. The House in Dunblane, a converted row of eighteenth century cottages opposite the Cathedral, was ecumenical. All the main-line Churches, except the Roman Catholic Church, contributed to its upkeep and running.

The sisters arrived in Dunblane in January, 1979, for a six-month trial period which was to last until 1994. Their main task was to promote prayer and spirituality, to develop a Retreat ministry, and to support the worship. Additional work for the sisters included acting as sub-wardens for SCH, greeting visitors, being there at meal-

Interior of the Chapel, 1983

times, running the bookshop, maintaining systems, and arranging flowers. It was a good mix, but there was also a factor of visibility within a community, for nuns are rare in Scotland, so that outreach was important.

Revised Horarium

Time	Event
6.00	Rise
6.20	Quiet Time*
7.15	Lauds
7.45	Eucharist**
8.15	Breakfast
	Work
12.40	Mid-day Office
1 pm	Dinner
	Work
4.00	Tea/recreation
5.30	Vespers
6.15	Supper
9.00	Compline

Greater Silence kept until the following morning

* some sisters do this later
** sometimes at 12.30

State of the Order in 1980

At the beginning of this decade Sister Janet was the Prioress and Sr Betty Sub-Prioress. There were 93 sisters in profession, many of whom were serving overseas. There were several novices.

Since 1960 there had been 48 professions, 28 sisters had left the Order and there had been 21 deaths – including that of the Foundress.

The next decade

The year 1980 saw two new houses open in England, one in Lancaster and one at Great Gaddesden in Hertfordshire where an individual sister led an experimental hermit-style life. After two sisters had undertaken courses in Lancaster a branch house was set up in 1980 for the Order to undertake parish work, and to work in Lancaster University Chaplaincy, building on earlier experience.

It was during the 1960s that quite radical alterations were made to the pattern of the Divine Office. Along with this went changes to the daily time-table and some modifications to the habit – wimples were out!

These two decades, 1960-1980, had seen many changes: they had encompassed the restlessness of the 'swinging sixties', coped with independence movements, the obscenity of apartheid and wars in Africa, and had passed through to the other side. The Order had seen the 1950s peak of vocations diminish, and experienced the secularisations that went with the uneasy times. They had coped with drastic shifts in education as examination systems changed, and new universities had made higher education more accessible to all, and they had done all this without Mother Margaret. Twenty-five of their number had died in profession, including all the founding sisters.

The Order had, in many ways, finally come of age.

Chapter 5   The End of the Millennium

Setting its sights on a Chronicle to lead to the end of the second millennium is a fitting act for a religious order, even if that order has been in existence for only a tiny fraction of that time. The concept of the religious life goes far back into the early centuries of the first millennium, and the Order of the Holy Paraclete is part of that long continuum. The world in which the Order functions has changed more dramatically in its short lifetime than in the nineteen centuries which preceded it, yet despite these changes, and in some cases because of them, the Order continues to fulfil its functions in religious and secular life. The present day may seem to have fulfilled Sr Mary Edith's fears, yet they have brought a great searching for spirituality, and if the influence of the Church may seem to have declined in this country, its burgeoning in Africa must be in no small measure due to the devoted work of those members of the Order whose 'love affair with Africa' has kept them in the heat and humidity of the tropics, and also of those sisters who have remained at the mother house maintaining the support systems that keep the Order functional.

West Africa

Although the Cape Coast house closed in 1976, and the house at Mampong finally closed in 1982, two sisters (one British, one Ghanaian) remained in Accra after handing over the school in 1980. The Ghanaian sister is still there, working with the Ghanaian church in a diversified ministry. Indeed, at the end of the millennium, a new initiative is planned for Ghana involving two young Ghanaian sisters; support is being sought from the wider church, to establish a new African community of Anglican Religious, 'to foster vocations, train novices and serve the church and local community'. Already in place are a large gift of land, from the Traditional Area Chief of Jachie in Ashanti, the support of the Diocese of Kumasi, and a network of past students, friends and associates.

The sisters have now been in Ghana for 75 years, and it says much for their work that it is a flourishing Ghanaian church which has this time invited their co-operation, rather than an English missionary bishop writing to the Church at home to beg for help in his work in the colonies.

Two good friends of the Order

Sr Judith greeting the Jachie Chief, donor of the land

Zimbabwe

The original definition of Southern Africa included what was then Rhodesia. However, that country, renamed Zimbabwe, became differentiated by the Church as a whole as part of the Province of Central Africa, and by the Order simply as a separate area of work. The sisters remained at the school at Bishopslea, in Harare, for five years, until the country had stabilised, and then in 1982 moved to another suburb, Cranborne, to start lay and Sunday School training schemes. This was again an **enabling** piece of work, and it followed the pattern of a diversified rather than an institutional ministry. The Order continued its work there until it finally left the new Zimbabwe in 1989, after 36 years.

Southern Africa

The Order has remained in South Africa until the present day, still managing St Benedict's House in Rosettenville, in the Johannesburg area. It functions as a retreat house, a conference centre and a day centre, providing a brief respite for people from areas such as the once notorious Soweto. African rule is in place, and apartheid is now only a hideous memory, though the Truth and Reconciliation Commission still regularly uncovers the worst of its effects. Nelson Mandela has retired, and the new government struggles with the problems of world economics in an increasingly unstable continent. Archbishop Desmond Tutu has remained a beacon of hope, courage and compassion recognised world-wide, and the team of sisters continues faithfully despite the increasing crime-wave. But then, they have never flinched for themselves.

In neighbouring Swaziland the sisters' presence continues, as the work which they originally undertook has become more diversified. No longer in St Michael's School, the sisters are working in industrial training centres and various church-based projects; one sister worked at the University and

Archbishop Desmond Tutu, an inspiration to millions and a good friend of OHP

another fulfilled the role of Diocesan Sunday School & Youth Worker. St Hilda's House, Manzini, opened in 1997 when the sisters finally left the St Michael's campus. From this house the sisters have extended their ministry by caring for children outside the traditional classroom. Most recently they have opened a 'shelter' for abused girls and AIDS victims, Jacaranda House.

The idea of setting up the industrial training centres emerged from a concern to offer help to youngsters who were either unable to afford high school education or who dropped out during the course and for whom there was no hope of training or employment. Sister Judith, the present Prioress, pioneered this work and with indefatigable zeal set about acquiring funds and staff to turn the idea into reality. The basic principle was (and remains) **training through production** and the centres earn about a third of their funds from the sale of goods and services. So successful was she in setting up the pilot scheme in Manzini that eventually the Government was convinced of the centre's usefulness and negotiated grants from the international community for further developments along the lines laid out by Sr Judith. Important local recognition of the value of this innovative project came in the form of an honorary doctorate from the University of Swaziland, conferred by the King in 1993.

Off to deliver carpentry products to a customer

Sr Judith also set up and encouraged the Swazi Kitchen, for the production of locally-made products such as chutney and marmalade, which are now sold world-wide through OXFAM. Such schemes are necessary to provide a culture of self-support. The money raised by the Swazi women's cookery funds a home for street children.

There is no longer a Sister Provincial for either West or Southern Africa; e-mail and fax machines mean that instant decisions, and helpful advice, can be sent from the Castle. Air travel means that no-one is more than a day away from home; a far cry from the long sea voyages and carts on dirt 'roads'.

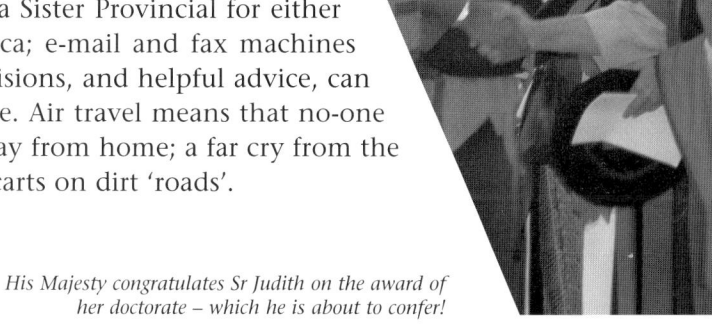

His Majesty congratulates Sr Judith on the award of her doctorate – which he is about to confer!

The Scottish Ventures

In Presbyterian Scotland the ecumenical ministry continued and even expanded. A series of sisters worked at Scottish Churches House in Dunblane until 1994, when shortage of numbers meant that they had to close that branch house. However, in 1996 the Order was asked to lend a sister to cover the lay sub-Warden's maternity leave, and so it was that Sr Dorothy Stella arrived in Dunblane just in time to help with the aftermath of the appalling Dunblane massacre, in which thirteen small children and their teacher were murdered, and many others injured. Though that stint ended with the return of the lay sub-Warden, there have been occasional return spells of work, without the formality of a branch house.

New ecumenical work in Scotland called, and three sisters went to live in a council flat in Dundee and to undertake various kinds of parish work and community service with a special emphasis on youth ministry, in this busy seaport city with all its attendant problems. This house was closed in September, 1999.

Northern Ireland

A further ecumenical call came to troubled Belfast. In 1986, a sister asked the Chapter for permission to go and live there as a member of the Columbanus Community of Reconciliation, a community of men and women from different denominations witnessing to Christian unity by their common life, while undertaking various kinds of work in the city. She was there from 1987 to 1990, and was then succeeded by another sister until 1993.

The State of the Order

It is easy in this secular and even anti-religious time to suggest that, at least in Britain, the religious life will die out. Indeed, many of the orders founded with such zeal in the nineteenth century have either closed or amalgamated, or have stopped accepting new members. Their prayerful work will not finish, but founded as so many of them were, to work with the poor and dispossessed, they have found their particular areas of ministry gone, lost with the coming of universal education, with the Health Service, with organised social work, with a new strength among native Christians in former colonies to which they could once go to preach the Word of God. It is those orders which have adapted to the changing times and have found new rôles that have survived, albeit with smaller numbers and often with an ageing population, but with minds willing to cope with new ideas.

The Order of the Holy Paraclete is such a survivor. The average age of the sisters is higher than it used to be, but women in the 21st century live longer than did their Victorian predecessors, and religious orders allow their members to work as long as they wish, and as they can. There is no compulsory retirement age in an order. Nor is there an enforced medical retirement for disability. As long as a sister feels she can offer something, even if it is only her wisdom and a listening ear, then she has a place. And when the time comes, she is cared for in the infirmary or in a nursing-home within reach of her sisters. The obligation of Life Profession works both ways, and has done so from the beginning. The sister working the high-tech switchboard and the computerised booking system for the Sneaton Castle Centre is well past pensionable age. The Chapter Clerk is only a bit younger, but surfs the web and the Order's collection of CD ROMS with youthful expertise.

> ### State of the Order in 2000
>
> *In this millennial year Sr Judith is the Prioress and Sr Barbara Ann the Sub-Prioress. There are 64 sisters in profession, nine of whom are stationed in Africa, and there are two novices.*
>
> *Since 1980 there have been 19 professions, while nine sisters have left the Order – some not renewing vows after first profession, others being released from life vows – and there have been 39 deaths (including the last of the OSMAA sisters)*

On the other hand, there are new vocations being tested and the two young novices with their white veils and cheerful enthusiasm foretell a good future. Fewer women come to test their vocations now, but of those few who are professed, more 'stick', and, as with much of the church, it is now a case of quality rather than quantity of adherents. That said, there are still over sixty professed sisters, working in Africa and in the UK. As one sister wrote, one of the advantages of the Order is that sisters can travel abroad, even if the bulk of their work is in the UK, to see how things are going, to cover a furlough, or just to provide a fresh face and new ideas.

English Diversity

Rievaulx remains as always, a facility for the Order where a sister may test her calling to a more contemplative life-style. Its connection goes too far back to the foundation for it to be lost. As always it is a House of Prayer. Great Gaddesden, however, has now closed.

The London house in Doughty Street closed down in 1987, but the Order was invited by the Archbishop of Canterbury to use a cottage in the grounds of Lambeth Palace, from which they were able to do such tasks as were required of them and to undertake outside ministry in the city. Most major church conferences take place in London, and the cottage was a useful base. However, that was given up in 1993, when one of the resident sisters was needed elsewhere. This still remains the Order's practice. It responds to the greatest need at the time.

Off to work – Lancaster style!

The work in Lancaster continued until well into 2000, although the branch house closed in 1994, for one sister had sought and gained permission to remain and carry on her work in the parish of Christ Church. A new house opened, however, in inner city Leicester, and continued from 1991 to 2000. The work was diverse within the city, though the house was a rather grand old Victorian vicarage, to the sisters' initial consternation. Newsletters and the *Millennium Miscellany* describe this work.

New work also began at Boston Spa, near Wetherby, in 1987, in setting up the Martin House Hospice for Children. Such work has developed alongside the hospice movement, and demands a special kind of dedication, not only for the OHP sisters, working with terminally sick children and their families. Sisters served on the care team and one acted as chaplain to the hospice.

The House was also home to one sister who worked in the chaplaincy at the Young Offenders' Institution (YOI), Wetherby. This again was a kind of return to the Order's earliest roots, with Mother Margaret's experience of penitent work in Wakefield prison with the sisters at Horbury. Now that others are continuing the work at Martin House, and the YOI, the branch house closed in May 2000.

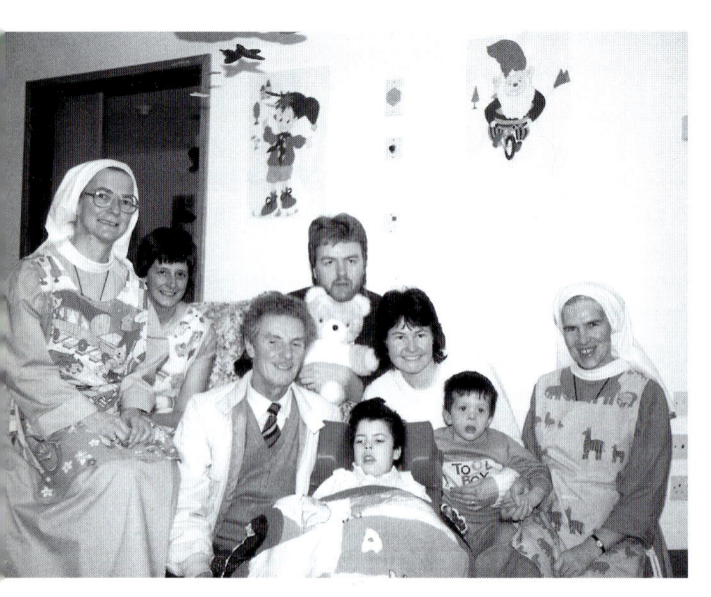

Martin House – children and carers

The work at the Minster in York continues, as the number of visitors and of school parties bent on national curriculum field-work continues to grow. The Minster is the mother church of the Diocese, and indeed of the Province, of York, and it is well that the Order, now the only one for women left in the Diocese, should be involved with the Minster's work. The dynamic has been left in the hands of the sisters from Whitby. Their work within the diocese extends beyond the Minster, since sisters sit on Parochial Church Councils, Deanery Synods, the Diocesan Synod and one is a member of General Synod.

The Mother House and St Hilda's School

What of the Castle at the end of the second millennium? A great deal has happened within the last twenty years. In 1986 the centenary of Mother Margaret's birth was commemorated with the building of a new school block for computer science and music. Indeed, life within the school was changing considerably. Over the years fewer sisters taught in the school, as they were called to other work, although a professed sister was always the Headmistress. The boarding element diminished and more day students were taken. The first boy pupils were admitted in 1981, and the school gradually became co-educational. The only previous boy pupil had been the single, un-named, small boy on whom Rupert Deakin had commented in 1918!

Woodlands was closed in 1987, and the preparatory school moved into Carr Hall to form an amalgamated lower school. The buildings were sold to become a private nursing home.

Meanwhile, in 1982 a nearby house had been bequeathed to the Order by Lady de Grimston, and opened in 1983 as St Oswald's Pastoral Centre, a facility which is of enormous value, both to the Whitby Deanery and to the wider community. Along with this has gone the development of a wider counselling and retreat-conducting ministry among the sisters.

St Oswald's Pastoral Centre

A second house, called Beachcliff, was opened in Whitby in 1987, on the sea front, and a group of older sisters lives there, linked with the parish and being generally visible within the community. Even walking Bracken, the dog, the current member of a long line of pets which have enjoyed the religious life ever since Peter the puppy shared the first Christmas dinner in 1915 is a kind of outreach.

In 1989 the Infirmary was extended once more, and in 1999 the bungalow opposite the Castle gate which had once been the Chaplain's residence and then served as guest accommodation was renamed Caedmon House and is home to three older sisters.

The farm continues to flourish, despite a current farming crisis reminiscent of the crisis of the 1930s which so troubled Mother Margaret. Pick-your-own fruit proved a popular venture, and brought the Order to the notice of local people, although, alas, it was not possible to find enough sisters to staff it, and it had to close. Now free-range eggs are proving a success, and the farm manager wins many prizes with the Priory's sheep and cattle at local shows.

In 1995 came a seismic change, when the last sister to be head of the School retired, and it was decided that a secular head should be appointed with a Board of Governors to include several sisters. This was done, with the newly secularised School leasing the school buildings, and becoming financially independent. Despite an initial endowment from the Order, the School ran into financial difficulties, and closed in 1997. It was a serious shock, for although the gap between Order and School had widened, and few sisters had been directly involved in running the school, the pupils had been a lively part of life at the Castle.

Sneaton Castle Centre

In 1998, after buying back the lease of St Hilda's School from the Administrators, the Chapter, after much prayer and thought, opened the Sneaton Castle Centre, to provide residential study facilities for school groups from the UK and overseas; for church groups; for university field-trips – Whitby is particularly popular with geology and marine biology departments – and for conferences. The Centre is run by a covenanted trading company, and there is now a shop, selling suitable merchandise, as well as religious and other books, and free-range eggs! The venture is proving a success, and has kept the Order in touch with education, even if their contact is not through teaching but through **enabling**, that all-important word. Several sisters are involved in the daily work of the Centre, and the Centre manager, Tony Holden, is a member of the Tertiary Order.

Sister Judith's long-standing work with the Duke of Edinburgh's Award Scheme, of which she is a Trustee, brought a happy private visit, in 1999, from the Duke of Edinburgh himself to see the Priory and the new Sneaton Castle Centre.

Into the Future

There are still new things happening, in addition to the development of the Centre, which has involved much carefully conceived rebuilding and refurbishment. Sr Rachel Clare has developed the Speedwell Project, for helping people to deal with severe and long-term pain. There is a new branch house in Hull, after a gap of 23 years, where three sisters live in the inner city parish of Sculcoates to undertake a varied ministry.

The Church of England voted to accept the ordination of women to the priesthood and Sr Marion Eva was among the first women ordained in 1994; she regularly celebrates the Eucharist in the Order, though a few sisters still find their consciences troubled by this development. A second sister is now training for the priesthood. The Order still has a male chaplain.

The sisters are not dull in their ways of doing things. One (a veteran of the evacuation to Canada, before her profession) recently did, with great gusto, a free-fall parachute jump in aid of charity; she had previously abseiled down the Castle tower! But then they never were dull at all; some of the earliest memories written of by pupils are of sisters tearing round hockey fields, their habits tucked up, and their red petticoats flapping in the wind. A recent *Newsletter* describes the encounter in 1999 of the Prioress and Sub-Prioress with a rhinoceros. The author's daughter has an abiding memory of one sister riding a moped with a crash-helmet over her veil, and moon-boots on her feet.

And, in 1999, the Order celebrated the diamond jubilee of profession of a sister who went to Canada with the evacuated school, and has served in many houses of the Order. After her great celebration she went off on a holiday with a niece in South America!

No, the sisters are not dull.

Abseiling down the tower

Bibliography

Booklets & Periodicals

Brief History of the Order of the Holy Paraclete, OHP
A History of Sneaton Castle, OHP
OHP Newsletter various editions
St Monica Calling various editions

Books

Sr Ethel Mary OHP, *Fulfilled in Joy*, Hodder and Stoughton, 1964

Anson, P., *The Call of the Cloister, Religious Communities and Kindred Bodies in the Anglican Communion*. (SPCK, 1956)

Chadwick, O., *The Victorian Church*, A. and C. Black, vol. 1, 3rd edn, 1970.

Chadwick, O., *The Victorian Church*, A. and C. Black, vol. 2, 2nd edn, 1972.

Curtis, S. J., *History of Education in Great Britain*, University Tutorial Press, 7th edn, 1967.

Graham, C. K., *The History of Education in Ghana*, Cass, 1971.

Hartington Jones, J., (ed.); *The German Attack on Scarborough*; Quoin Publishing, 1989.

Hattersley, R., *Blood and Fire*, Little Brown, 1999.

Horrell, M., *A Decade of Bantu Education*, South African Institute of Race Relations, 1964.

Howard-Bennett, R., *I Choose the Cloister*; Hodder and Stoughton, 1956.

Marcum, J. A., *Education, Race and Social Change in South Africa*, University of California Press, 1982.

Mumm, S., *Stolen Daughters, Virgin Mothers*; Leicester U. P., 1999.

OHP Sisters, *Millennium Miscellany*, OHP, Whitby, 2000.

Parker, F., *African Development and education in Southern Rhodesia*, Ohio State UP, 1960.

Penniston, J., *The Church in Whitby, 1875-1985*, Whitby PCC, 1986.

Prioress of Whitby, *Archbishop Garbett*; Mowbray, 1957.

Documents

Reminiscences from sisters, former sisters, pupils and others.
Archive of the Order of the Holy Paraclete (uncatalogued).

Appendix I

Rupert Deakin's **'Further Details'** section on the state of the school.
It is written neatly in long-hand on thick blue foolscap paper.

St Hilda's School has been recognised by the Cambridge University Syndicate as a training department for secondary teachers.
Each pupil is examined at the beginning of the first term and periodically afterwards by the Medical officer who attends the school and regulates the children's dietary [needs] and the amount of time to be spent on games, swimming and study. The priest-in-charge of St Ninian's acts as school chaplain.

The Castle contains:-
In the basement:- Music room, Kitchen, scullery, larder, strong room and store room.
On the ground floor:- Large entrance hall which is used as a place of assembly, classroom for Form Remove, drawing room, dining room, and staff library.
On the first floor:- Classrooms for Forms VI, V, III, and II, dormitory with 9 beds for young children, community room, bathroom, and lavatory.
On the second floor:- Sitting room, four small bedrooms, another bedroom; and in the tower, the chapel.
The new buildings, now in the course of completion, will contain a dormitory, and four bathrooms, and lavatories.
(Different hand) There is no laboratory and no art room.
The Castle is lighted by electricity; the rooms and corridors are heated by radiators, electric stoves, and open fires. The grounds contain two tennis courts, a junior playing field, a hockey field, and about 1½ acres of Kitchen garden.
The annual rent of the Castle is £190
A group of out-buildings did not seem to be used except for teaching Form IV and some music.

The Lodge contains a students' sitting-room, and four bedrooms for students and one mistress.

The Manor House contains 13 bedrooms, a Kitchen, two rooms for mistresses, a staff-room and a bathroom. There is a tennis court in the grounds. The rent for the manor House is £55.

Fees:-		
	Boarders under 12 years of age	£40 a year
	14	£45
	over 14	from £50 to £70 a year
	Day Pupils under 7 years of age	1½ guineas per term
	from 7 to 12	2½ guineas per term
	over 12	4 guineas per term
	Entrance fee, half a guinea	

Special terms are made for sisters and children of the clergy.
Mr Deakin reported that there were 60 girls and one small boy in the school, a fair increase upon the 39 who joined at the start of 1915. The teaching was undertaken by the Prioress and five other members of the order, with four or more resident mistresses and several students and senior girls. Mr Deakin described it as a strong staff. It was certainly an enviable pupil-teacher ratio.

Appendix II

From the Day-Book for 1940

Monday, June 17 Collapse of France. At Conference after dinner as an informal emergency Chapter – decided to evacuate school to Canada. First steps taken immediately The Bugthorpe Sisters came for a week's holiday.

Tuesday, June 18 'Packing Day' – packed what was thought to be necessary for evacuation. Letters, Cables, telegrams, 'phone calls began. School went on as usual. Sister Mary Edith returned from the Cottage where she had been staying with Sr Mary Hilda since her illness. Passport photographs taken by Mr Kettle.

June 19 Complications & difficulties began. At 10 minutes notice Sr Monica & Sr Elsa went to London to struggle with business arrangements. A school group was taken by Mr Kettle.

June 20 School went on as usual with regular work somewhat disorganised. Everyone very busy. News of evacuation spreading & applications began to come in.

June 21 Still more busy. Parents arrived & many were most helpful with packing etc. Annexe full of packing cases: hall full of trunks – parents everywhere.

June 22 Passports & permits dealt with. Children sorted out. No evacuation allowed for over '16s'. Later in the day a house near Middleton in Teesdale was secured by the help of Mr Farndale to accommodate members of the school not going to Canada. Also today military came to requisition the buildings & grounds. Sr Monica & Sr Elsa returned from London on 7.10 train. Meanwhile Sr Kathleen had gone to London.

Sunday, June 23 an unusual Sunday – more parents. Many new children [younger siblings, including small boys, were evacuated with the children]. Medical examination – Junior 10.20 & Senior 11.0 Services as usual but no Junior 5 o'clock. Except short prayers with Sr Bridget Mary – No social gathering in Common Room for coffee at 11.30 a.m. & no afternoon social cup of tea with staff. Mass was very special – hymn 470 & Procession down Chapel afterwards. A terrible feeling of 'the last time' – In the afternoon Mother had unpleasant interview with the billeting officer – then she went to Whitby to interview the Brigadier General & it was settled that our household of 180-200 would not be turned out of their beds this night.

Monday, June 24 – St John the Baptist's day. In spite of upheaval we all sat down for Community Lunch for half an hour. At midday the lorries went off to Liverpool with cases & trunks. The drive & front field today was a mixture of children & military & military lorries & parents' cars stood side by side. At 6.30 tea there was a farewell Service in Chapel which was literally packed tight. Fr Armitstead read the Archbishop's message to the school – the *Te Deum* was sung. The Sisters returned to Bugthorpe. Mother gave the Sisters a special Address after Compline.

Tuesday, June 25 – Evacuation Day. Mass 6 o'clock in the Oratory – for Sisters going to Canada. Mass 7 o'clock in Chapel for the rest of us – as the Middleton group were also making an early start. 7.30 am – 3 transport buses started for Liverpool with 100 children & 10 adults (Sr Gertrude, Sr Monica, Sr Lilian, Sr Daisy, Sr Elsa, Sr Marguerite, Miss Healey, Miss Taylor, Miss Wills, M Ruddle) Mother & Sr Anne went to see them off. At 9.20 – 2 more bus loads went to Wemmergill Hall, Nr Middleton.

Wednesday, June 26 Mother saw the children on to the boat at Liverpool – at 4 pm. At home very busy cleaning & tidying up. Brigadier-General called & expressed desire to occupy Castle & kitchens Thursday or Friday – Drive, edge of field full of buses, vans & cars, San. Field occupied – also san. & telephone. Soldiers trespassed in the hay & in the paddock occupied by the bull! In the afternoon of this day the Sisters & Novices set to work to move contents of store-cupboard & kitchen – to Novices' 'lobby'.

June 27 Stripping of all rooms in the castle – except drawing-room & Common-room. Soldiers helped with heavy furniture. Mrs Hugill prepared meals in stripped kitchen. Telephoning today was almost impossible Mother & Sr Anne returned from Liverpool.

June 28 Stripping continued – then a sudden message 'don't do any more – message from War Office to say do not occupy Sneaton Castle' !! telephone restored.

June 29 S Peter's Day – Sung Mass. Settlement between Mother & the Brigadier-General & soldiers were to have the san. Field, Dormitories & Bungalow. Fr Armitstead went to Middleton – taking with him necessities for Chapel there. Fr Millard arrived. All maids left except Mrs Hugill & the Woods.

Sunday, June 30 Mother & Sr Anne went to Middleton & returned at 9 pm.

July 1 Mother went to London on evacuation business. Sr Mary Edith & Sr Anne very busy with correspondence re second batch to go to Canada. 1st Vespers of the Visitation – just as usual though very few Sisters.

July 2 Feast of the Visitation. Sung Mass; Sr Mary Edith played the organ. Mother away but returned at supper time. Fr Horner arrived at midday to hear Confessions. Fr Millard went after breakfast.

July 3 Fr Horner went. Canadian business correspondence very heavy. 3 voluntary typists came to help.

July 4 heard of the safe arrival of our children in Canadian waters. Fr Heppenstall came.

July 5 Sr Kathleen went on another visit to London to deal with business at the Passport Office.

July 7 (Sunday) Mother, Sr Mary Edith & Sr Anne went to Middleton – returned at 9 pm.

July 10 – This was the day which was to have been the Welfare Fête if things had been normal. Thunder & Lightning & torrential rain!

July 11 Fr Heppenstall & the Army Chaplain arranged school refectory as a Soldiers' rest-room & canteen.

July 13 Sr Winifred came from Hessle, Mrs Healey came to give Sr Mary Edith Massage treatment.

July 14 (Sunday) – Canteen began to work. 9.45 am 180 soldiers tried to get into Chapel for Church Parade – Extra chairs & benches brought in, but many soldiers had to be turned away.

July 15 Date of second sailing postponed till Saturday. Sr Kathleen again went to London – First letters arrived from Canada (written on the voyage).

Tuesday, July 16 6.30 pm message came to say boat sailing Thursday not Saturday. All arrangements rearranged at 11th hour – 'phoning till almost midnight.

Wednesday, July 17 Mother & Sr Anne started in transport bus at 7 am to collect children from Middleton. They spent the night at Rankin Hall, Liverpool.

July 18 Children embarked – after vast difficulties (Sr Bridget Mary, Miss Poynton, Miss Williams, Miss Crabtree & J. Roberts in charge) (they did not sail out of the Mersey until Sunday night owing to the enemy's mine-laying).

July 20 A big batch of letters from Canada + cuttings from Canadian newspapers…

Monday, July 29 All Sisters started to clean the Castle from top to bottom. Today we heard of the safe arrival of the second batch of children in Canada.